Locrine
A Tragedy

Algernon Charles Swinburne

Contents

LOCRINE
A TRAGEDY

BY

Algernon Charles Swinburne

DEDICATION
TO ALICE SWINBURNE.

LOCRINE--A TRAGEDY
by Algernon Charles Swinburne

I.

The love that comes and goes like wind or fire
Hath words and wings wherewith to speak and flee.
But love more deep than passion's deep desire,
Clear and inviolable as the unsounded sea,
What wings of words may serve to set it free,
To lift and lead it homeward? Time and death
Are less than love: or man's live spirit saith
False, when he deems his life is more than breath.

II.

No words may utter love; no sovereign song
Speak all it would for love's sake. Yet would I
Fain cast in moulded rhymes that do me wrong
Some little part of all my love: but why
Should weak and wingless words be fain to fly?
For us the years that live not are not dead:
Past days and present in our hearts are wed:
My song can say no more than love hath said.

III.

Love needs nor song nor speech to say what love
Would speak or sing, were speech and song not weak
To bear the sense-belated soul above
And bid the lips of silence breathe and speak.
Nor power nor will has love to find or seek
Words indiscoverable, ampler strains of song
Than ever hailed him fair or shewed him strong:
And less than these should do him worse than wrong.

IV.

We who remember not a day wherein
We have not loved each other,--who can see
No time, since time bade first our days begin,
Within the sweep of memory's wings, when we
Have known not what each other's love must be, -
We are well content to know it, and rest on this,
And call not words to witness that it is.
To love aloud is oft to love amiss.

V.

But if the gracious witness borne of words
Take not from speechless love the secret grace
That binds it round with silence, and engirds
Its heart with memories fair as heaven's own face,
Let love take courage for a little space
To speak and be rebuked not of the soul,
Whose utterance, ere the unwitting speech be whole,
Rebukes itself, and craves again control.

VI.

A ninefold garland wrought of song-flowers nine
Wound each with each in chance-inwoven accord
Here at your feet I lay as on a shrine
Whereof the holiest love that lives is lord.
With faint strange hues their leaves are freaked and scored:
The fable-flowering land wherein they grew
Hath dreams for stars, and grey romance for dew:
Perchance no flower thence plucked may flower anew.

VII.

No part have these wan legends in the sun
Whose glory lightens Greece and gleams on Rome.
Their elders live: but these--their day is done,
Their records written of the wind in foam
Fly down the wind, and darkness takes them home.
What Homer saw, what Virgil dreamed, was truth,
And dies not, being divine: but whence, in sooth,
Might shades that never lived win deathless youth?

VIII.

The fields of fable, by the feet of faith
Untrodden, bloom not where such deep mist drives.
Dead fancy's ghost, not living fancy's wraith,
Is now the storied sorrow that survives
Faith in the record of these lifeless lives.
Yet Milton's sacred feet have lingered there,
His lips have made august the fabulous air,
His hands have touched and left the wild weeds fair.

IX.

So, in some void and thought-untrammelled hour,
Let these find grace, my sister, in your sight,
Whose glance but cast on casual things hath power
To do the sun's work, bidding all be bright
With comfort given of love: for love is light.
Were all the world of song made mine to give,
The best were yours of all its flowers that live:
Though least of all be this my gift, forgive.

July 1887.

PERSONS REPRESENTED.

LOCRINE, King of Britain.
CAMBER, King of Wales, brother to LOCRINE.
MADAN, son to LOCRINE and GUENDOLEN.
DEBON, Lord Chamberlain.

GUENDOLEN, Queen of Britain, cousin and wife to LOCRINE.
ESTRILD, a German princess, widow of the Scythian king HUMBER.
SABRINA, daughter to LOCRINE and ESTRILD.

Scene, BRITAIN.

ACT I.

SCENE I.--Troynovant. A Room in the Palace.

Enter GUENDOLEN and MADAN.

GUENDOLEN.

Child, hast thou looked upon thy grandsire dead?

MADAN.

Ay.

GUENDOLEN.

Then thou sawest our Britain's heart and head
Death-stricken. Seemed not there my sire to thee
More great than thine, or all men living? We
Stand shadows of the fathers we survive:
Earth bears no more nor sees such births alive.

MADAN.

Why, he was great of thews--and wise, thou say'st:
Yet seems my sire to me the fairer-faced -
The kinglier and the kindlier.

GUENDOLEN.

Yea, his eyes
Are liker seas that feel the summering skies
In concord of sweet colour--and his brow
Shines gentler than my father's ever: thou,
So seeing, dost well to hold thy sire so dear.

MADAN.

I said not that his love sat yet so near
My heart as thine doth: rather am I thine,
Thou knowest, than his.

GUENDOLEN.

Nay--rather seems Locrine
Thy sire than I thy mother.

MADAN.

Wherefore?

GUENDOLEN.

Boy,
Because of all our sires who fought for Troy

Most like thy father and my lord Locrine,
I think, was Paris.

MADAN.

How may man divine
Thy meaning? Blunt am I, thou knowest, of wit;
And scarce yet man--men tell me.

GUENDOLEN.

Ask not it.
I meant not thou shouldst understand--I spake
As one that sighs, to ease her heart of ache,
And would not clothe in words her cause for sighs -
Her naked cause of sorrow.

MADAN.

Wert thou wise,
Mother, thy tongue had chosen of two things one -
Silence, or speech.

GUENDOLEN.

Speech had I chosen, my son,
I had wronged thee--yea, perchance I have wronged thine ears
Too far, to say so much.

MADAN.

Nay, these are tears
That gather toward thine eyelids now. Thou hast broken

Silence--if now thy speech die down unspoken,
Thou dost me wrong indeed--but more than mine
The wrong thou dost thyself is.

GUENDOLEN.

And Locrine -
Were not thy sire wronged likewise of me?

MADAN.

Yea.

GUENDOLEN.

Yet--I may choose yet--nothing will I say
More.

MADAN.

Choose, and have thy choice; it galls not me.

GUENDOLEN.

Son, son! thy speech is bitterer than the sea.

MADAN.

Yet, were the gulfs of hell not bitterer, thine
Might match thy son's, who hast called my sire--Locrine -
Thy lord, and lord of all this land--the king
Whose name is bright and sweet as earth in spring,
Whose love is mixed with Britain's very life

As heaven with earth at sunrise--thou, his wife,
Hast called him--and the poison of the word
Set not thy tongue on fire--I lived and heard -
Coward.

GUENDOLEN.

Thou liest.

MADAN.

If then thy speech rang true,
Why, now it rings not false.

GUENDOLEN.

Thou art treacherous too -
His heart, thy father's very heart is thine -
O, well beseems it, meet it is, Locrine,
That liar and traitor and changeling he should be
Who, though I bare him, was begot by thee.

MADAN.

How have I lied, mother? Was this the lie,
That thou didst call my father coward, and I
Heard?

GUENDOLEN.

Nay--I did but liken him with one
Not all unlike him; thou, my child, his son,
Art more unlike thy father.

MADAN.

Was not then,
Of all our fathers, all recorded men,
The man whose name, thou sayest, is like his name -
Paris--a sign in all men's mouths of shame?

GUENDOLEN.

Nay, save when heaven would cross him in the fight,
He bare him, say the minstrels, as a knight -
Yea, like thy father.

MADAN.

Shame then were it none
Though men should liken me to him?

GUENDOLEN.

My son,
I had rather see thee--see thy brave bright head,
Strong limbs, clear eyes--drop here before me dead.

MADAN.

If he were true man, wherefore?

GUENDOLEN.

False was he;
No coward indeed, but faithless, trothless--we
Hold therefore, as thou sayest, his princely name

Unprincely--dead in honour--quick in shame.

MADAN.

And his to mine thou likenest?

GUENDOLEN.

Thine? to thine?
God rather strike thy life as dark as mine
Than tarnish thus thine honour! For to me
Shameful it seems--I know not if it be -
For men to lie, and smile, and swear, and lie,
And bear the gods of heaven false witness. I
Can hold not this but shameful.

MADAN.

Thou dost well.
I had liefer cast my soul alive to hell
Than play a false man false. But were he true
And I the traitor--then what heaven should do
I wot not, but myself, being once awake
Out of that treasonous trance, were fain to slake
With all my blood the fire of shame wherein
My soul should burn me living in my sin.

GUENDOLEN.

Thy soul? Yea, there--how knowest thou, boy, so well? -
The fire is lit that feeds the fires of hell.
Mine is aflame this long time now--but thine -
O, how shall God forgive thee this, Locrine,

That thou, for shame of these thy treasons done,
Hast rent the soul in sunder of thy son?

MADAN.

My heart is whole yet, though thy speech be fire
Whose flame lays hold upon it. Hath my sire
Wronged thee?

GUENDOLEN.

Nay, child, I lied--I did but rave -
I jested--was my face, then, sad and grave,
When most I jested with thee? Child, my brain
Is wearied, and my heart worn down with pain:
I thought awhile, for very sorrow's sake,
To play with sorrow--try thy spirit, and take
Comfort--God knows I know not what I said,
My father, whom I loved, being newly dead.

MADAN.

I pray thee that thou jest with me no more
Thus.

GUENDOLEN.

Dost thou now believe me?

MADAN.

No.

GUENDOLEN.

I bore
A brave man when I bore thee.

MADAN.

I desire
No more of laud or leasing. Hath my sire
Wronged thee?

GUENDOLEN.

Never. But wilt thou trust me now?

MADAN.

As trustful am I, mother of mine, as thou.

Enter LOCRINE.

LOCRINE.

The gods be good to thee! How farest thou?

GUENDOLEN.

Well.
Heaven hath no power to hurt me more: and hell
No fire to fear. The world I dwelt in died
With my dead father. King, thy world is wide
Wherein thy soul rejoicingly puts trust:
But mine is strait, and built by death of dust.

LOCRINE.

Thy sire, mine uncle, stood the sole man, then,
That held thy life up happy? Guendolen,
Hast thou nor child nor husband--or are we
Worth no remembrance more at all of thee?

GUENDOLEN.

Thy speech is sweet; thine eyes are flowers that shine:
If ever siren bare a son, Locrine,
To reign in some green island and bear sway
On shores more shining than the front of day
And cliffs whose brightness dulls the morning's brow,
That son of sorceries and of seas art thou.

LOCRINE.

Nay, now thy tongue it is that plays on men;
And yet no siren's honey, Guendolen,
Is this fair speech, though soft as breathes the south,
Which thus I kiss to silence on thy mouth.

GUENDOLEN.

Thy soul is softer than this boy's of thine:
His heart is all toward battle. Was it mine
That put such fire in his? for none that heard
Thy flatteries--nay, I take not back the word -
A flattering lover lives my loving lord -
Could guess thine hand so great with spear or sword.

LOCRINE.

What have I done for thee to mock with praise
And make the boy's eyes widen? All my days
Are worth not all a week, if war be all,
Of his that loved no bloodless festival -
Thy sire, and sire of slaughters: this was one
Who craved no more of comfort from the sun
But light to lighten him toward battle: I
Love no such life as bids men kill or die.

GUENDOLEN.

Wert thou not woman more in word than act,
Then unrevenged thy brother Albanact
Had given his blood to guard his realm and thine:
But he that slew him found thy stroke, Locrine,
Strong as thy speech is gentle.

LOCRINE.

God assoil
The dead our friends and foes!

GUENDOLEN.

A goodly spoil
Was that thine hand made then by Humber's banks
Of all who swelled the Scythian's riotous ranks
With storm of inland surf and surge of steel:
None there were left, if tongues ring true, to feel
The yoke of days that breathe submissive breath
More bitter than the bitterest edge of death.

LOCRINE.

None.

GUENDOLEN.

This was then a day of blood. I heard,
But know not whence I caught the wandering word,
Strange women were there of that outland crew,
Whom ruthlessly thy soldiers ravening slew.

LOCRINE.

Nay, Scythians then had we been, worse than they.

GUENDOLEN.

These that were taken, then, thou didst not slay?

LOCRINE.

I did not say we spared them.

GUENDOLEN.

Slay nor spare?

LOCRINE.

How if they were not?

GUENDOLEN.

What albeit they were?
Small hurt, meseems, my husband, had it been
Though British hands had haled a Scythian queen -
If such were found--some woman foul and fierce -
To death--or aught we hold for shame's sake worse.

LOCRINE.

For shame's own sake the hand that should not fear
To take such monstrous work upon it here,
And did not wither from the wrist, should be
Hewn off ere hanging. Wolves or men are we,
That thou shouldst question this?

GUENDOLEN.

Not wolves, but men,
Surely: for beasts are loyal.

LOCRINE.

Guendolen,
What irks thee?

GUENDOLEN.

Nought save grief and love; Locrine,
A grievous love, a loving grief is mine.
Here stands my husband: there my father lies:
I know not if there live in either's eyes
More love, more life of comfort. This our son

Loves me: but is there else left living one
That loves me back as I love?

LOCRINE.

Nay, but how
Has this wild question fired thine heart?

GUENDOLEN.

Not thou!
No part have I--nay, never had I part -
Our child that hears me knows it--in thine heart.
Thy sire it was that bade our hands be one
For love of mine, his brother: thou, his son,
Didst give not--no--but yield thy hand to mine,
To mine thy lips--not thee to me, Locrine.
Thy heart has dwelt far off me all these years;
Yet have I never sought with smiles or tears
To lure or melt it meward. I have borne -
I that have borne to thee this boy--thy scorn,
Thy gentleness, thy tender words that bite
More deep than shame would, shouldst thou spurn or smite
These limbs and lips made thine by contract--made
No wife's, no queen's--a servant's--nay, thy shade.
The shadow am I, my lord and king, of thee,
Who art spirit and substance, body and soul to me.
And now,--nay, speak not--now my sire is dead
Thou think'st to cast me crownless from thy bed
Wherein I brought thee forth a son that now
Shall perish with me, if thou wilt--and thou
Shalt live and laugh to think of us--or yet
Play faith more foul--play falser, and forget.

LOCRINE.

Sharp grief has crazed thy brain. Thou knowest of me -

GUENDOLEN.

I know that nought I know, Locrine, of thee.

LOCRINE.

What bids thee then revile me, knowing no cause?

GUENDOLEN.

Strong sorrow knows but sorrow's lawless laws.

LOCRINE.

Yet these should turn not grief to raging fire.

GUENDOLEN.

They should not, had my heart my heart's desire.

LOCRINE.

Would God that love, my queen, could give thee this!

GUENDOLEN.

Thou dost not call me wife--nor call'st amiss.

LOCRINE.

What name should serve to stay this fitful strife?

GUENDOLEN.

Thou dost not ill to call me not thy wife.

LOCRINE.

My sister wellnigh wast thou once: and now -

GUENDOLEN.

Thy sister never I: my brother thou.

LOCRINE.

How shall man sound this riddle? Read it me.

GUENDOLEN.

As loves a sister, never loved I thee.

LOCRINE.

Not when we played as twinborn child with child?

GUENDOLEN.

If then thou thought'st it, both were sore beguiled.

LOCRINE.

I thought thee sweeter then than summer doves.

GUENDOLEN.

Yet not like theirs--woe worth it!--were our loves.

LOCRINE.

No--for they meet and flit again apart.

GUENDOLEN.

And we live linked, inseparate--heart in heart.

LOCRINE.

Is this the grief that wrings and vexes thine?

GUENDOLEN.

Thy mother laughed when thou wast born, Locrine.

LOCRINE.

Did she not well? sweet laughter speaks not scorn.

GUENDOLEN.

And thou didst laugh, and wept'st not, to be born.

LOCRINE.

Did I then ill? didst thou, then, weep to be?

GUENDOLEN.

The same star lit not thee to birth and me.

LOCRINE.

Thine eyes took light, then, from the fairer star.

GUENDOLEN.

Nay; thine was nigh the sun, and mine afar.

LOCRINE.

Too bright was thine to need the neighbouring sun.

GUENDOLEN.

Nay, all its life of light was wellnigh done.

LOCRINE.

If all on thee its light and life were shed
And darkness on thy birthday struck it dead,
It died most happy, leaving life and light
More fair and full in loves more thankful sight.

GUENDOLEN.

Art thou so thankful, king, for love's kind sake?
Would I were worthier thanks like these I take!
For thanks I cannot render thee again.

LOCRINE.

Too heavy sits thy sorrow, Guendolen,
Upon thy spirit of life: I bid thee not
Take comfort while the fire of grief is hot
Still at thine heart, and scarce thy last keen tear
Dried: yet the gods have left thee comfort here.

GUENDOLEN.

Comfort? In thee, fair cousin--or my son?

LOCRINE.

What hast thou done, Madan, or left undone?
Toward thee and me thy mother's mood to-day
Seems less than loving.

MADAN.

Sire, I cannot say.

LOCRINE.

Enough: an hour or half an hour is more
Than wrangling words should stuff with barren store.
Comfort may'st thou bring to her, if I may none,

When all her father quickens in her son.
In Cornish warfare if thou win thee praise,
Thine shall men liken to thy grandsire's days.

GUENDOLEN.

To Cornwall must he fare and fight for thee?

LOCRINE.

If heart be his--and if thy will it be.

GUENDOLEN.

What is my will worth more than wind or foam?

LOCRINE.

Why, leave is thine to hold him here at home.

GUENDOLEN.

What power is mine to speed him or to stay?

LOCRINE.

None--should thy child cast love and shame away.

GUENDOLEN.

Most duteous wast thou to thy sire--and mine.

LOCRINE.

Yea, truly--when their bidding sealed me thine.

GUENDOLEN.

Thy smile is as a flame that plays and flits.

LOCRINE.

Yet at my heart thou knowest what fire there sits.

GUENDOLEN.

Not love's--not love's--toward me love burns not there.

LOCRINE.

What wouldst thou have me search therein and swear?

GUENDOLEN.

Swear by the faith none seeking there may find -

LOCRINE.

Then--by the faith that lives not in thy kind -

GUENDOLEN.

Ay--women's faith is water. Then, by men's -

LOCRINE.

Yea--by Locrine's, and not by Guendolen's -

GUENDOLEN.

Swear thou didst never love me more than now.

LOCRINE.

I swear it--not when first we kissed. And thou?

GUENDOLEN.

I cannot give thee back thine oath again.

LOCRINE.

If now love wane within thee, lived it then?

GUENDOLEN.

I said not that it waned. I would not swear -

LOCRINE.

That it was ever more than shadows were?

GUENDOLEN.

- Thy faith and heart were aught but shadow and fire.

LOCRINE.

But thou, meseems, hast loved--thy son and sire.

GUENDOLEN.

And not my lord: I cross and thwart him still.

LOCRINE.

Thy grief it is that wounds me--not thy will.

GUENDOLEN.

Wound? if I would, could I forsooth wound thee?

LOCRINE.

I think thou wouldst not, though thine hands were free.

GUENDOLEN.

These hands, now bound in wedlock fast to thine?

LOCRINE.

Yet were thine heart not then dislinked from mine.

GUENDOLEN.

Nay, life nor death, nor love whose child is hate,
May sunder hearts made one but once by fate.
Wrath may come down as fire between them--life

May bid them yearn for death as man for wife -
Grief bid them stoop as son to father--shame
Brand them, and memory turn their pulse to flame -
Or falsehood change their blood to poisoned wine -
Yet all shall rend them not in twain, Locrine.

LOCRINE.

Who knows not this? but rather would I know
What thought distempers and distunes thy woe.
I came to wed my grief awhile to thine
For love's sake and for comfort's -

GUENDOLEN.

Thou, Locrine?
Today thou knowest not, nor wilt learn tomorrow,
The secret sense of such a word as sorrow.
Thy spirit is soft and sweet: I well believe
Thou wouldst, but well I know thou canst not grieve.
The tears like fire, the fire that burns up tears,
The blind wild woe that seals up eyes and ears,
The sound of raging silence in the brain
That utters things unutterable for pain,
The thirst at heart that cries on death for ease,
What knows thy soul's live sense of pangs like these?

LOCRINE.

Is no love left thee then for comfort?

GUENDOLEN.

Thine?

LOCRINE.

Thy son's may serve thee, though thou mock at mine.

GUENDOLEN.

Ay--when he comes again from Cornwall.

LOCRINE.

Nay;
If now his absence irk thee, bid him stay.

GUENDOLEN. -

I will not--yea, I would not, though I might.
Go, child: God guard and grace thine hand in fight!

MADAN.

My heart shall give it grace to guard my head.

LOCRINE.

Well thought, my son: but scarce of thee well said.

MADAN.

No skill of speech have I: words said or sung

Help me no more than hand is helped of tongue:
Yet, would some better wit than mine, I wis,
Help mine, I fain would render thanks for this.

GUENDOLEN.

Think not the boy I bare thee too much mine,
Though slack of speech and halting: I divine
Thou shalt not find him faint of heart or hand,
Come what may come against him.

LOCRINE.

Nay, this land
Bears not alive, nor bare it ere we came,
Such bloodless hearts as know not fame from shame,
Or quail for hope's sake, or more faithless fear,
From truth of single-sighted manhood, here
Born and bred up to read the word aright
That sunders man from beast as day from night.
That red rank Ireland where men burn and slay
Girls, old men, children, mothers, sires, and say
These wolves and swine that skulk and strike do well,
As soon might know sweet heaven from ravenous hell.

GUENDOLEN.

Ay: no such coward as crawls and licks the dust
Till blood thence licked may slake his murderous lust
And leave his tongue the suppler shall be bred,
I think, in Britain ever--if the dead
May witness for the living. Though my son
Go forth among strange tribes to battle, none

Here shall he meet within our circling seas
So much more vile than vilest men as these.
And though the folk be fierce that harbour there
As once the Scythians driven before thee were,
And though some Cornish water change its name
As Humber then for furtherance of thy fame,
And take some dead man's on it--some dead king's
Slain of our son's hand--and its watersprings
Wax red and radiant from such fire of fight
And swell as high with blood of hosts in flight -
No fiercer foe nor worthier shall he meet
Than then fell grovelling at his father's feet.
Nor, though the day run red with blood of men
As that whose hours rang round thy praises then,
Shall thy son's hand be deeper dipped therein
Than his that gat him--and that held it sin
To spill strange blood of barbarous women--wives
Or harlots--things of monstrous names and lives -
Fit spoil for swords of harsher-hearted folk;
Nor yet, though some that dared and 'scaped the stroke
Be fair as beasts are beauteous,--fit to make
False hearts of fools bow down for love's foul sake,
And burn up faith to ashes--shall my son
Forsake his father's ways for such an one
As whom thy soldiers slew or slew not--thou
Hast no remembrance of them left thee now.
Even therefore may we stand assured of this:
What lip soever lure his lip to kiss,
Past question--else were he nor mine nor thine -
This boy would spurn a Scythian concubine.

LOCRINE.

Such peril scarce may cross or charm our son,
Though fairer women earth or heaven sees none
Than those whose breath makes mild our wild south-west
Where now he fares not forth on amorous quest.

GUENDOLEN.

Wilt thou not bless him going, and bid him speed?

LOCRINE.

So be it: yet surely not in word but deed
Lives all the soul of blessing or of ban
Or wrought or won by manhood's might for man.
The gods be gracious to thee, boy, and give
Thy wish its will!

MADAN.

So shall they, if I live.
[Exeunt.

SCENE II.--Gardens of the Palace.

Enter CAMBER and DEBON.

CAMBER.

Nay, tell not me: no smoke of lies can smother
The truth which lightens through thy lies: I see
Whose trust it is that makes a liar of thee,
And how thy falsehood, man, has faith for mother.
What, is not thine the breast wherein my brother
Seals all his heart up? Had he put in me
Faith--but his secret has thy tongue for key,
And all his counsel opens to none other.
Thy tongue, thine eye, thy smile unlocks his trust
Who puts no trust in man.

DEBON.

Sir, then were I
A traitor found more perfect fool than knave
Should I play false, or turn for gold to dust
A gem worth all the gold beneath the sky -
The diamond of the flawless faith he gave
Who sealed his trust upon me.

CAMBER.

What art thou?
Because thy beard ere mine were black was grey
Art thou the prince, and I thy man? I say

Thou shalt not keep his counsel from me.

DEBON.

Now,
Prince, may thine old born servant lift his brow
As from the dust to thine, and answer--Nay.
Nor canst thou turn this nay of mine to yea
With all the lightning of thine eyes, I trow,
Nor this my truth to treason.

CAMBER.

God us aid!
Art thou not mad? Thou knowest what whispers crawl
About the court with serpent sound and speed,
Made out of fire and falsehood; or if made
Not all of lies--it may be thus--not all -
Black yet no less with poison.

DEBON.

Prince, indeed
I know the colour of the tongues of fire
That feed on shame to slake the thirst of hate;
Hell-black, and hot as hell: nor age nor state
May pluck the fangs forth of their foul desire:
I that was trothplight servant to thy sire,
A king more kingly than the front of fate
That bade our lives bow down disconsolate
When death laid hold on him--for hope nor hire,
Prince, would I lie to thee: nay, what avails
Falsehood? thou knowest I would not.

CAMBER.

Why, thou art old;
To thee could falsehood bear but fruitless fruit -
Lean grafts and sour. I think thou wouldst not.

DEBON.

Wales
In such a lord lives happy: young and bold
And yet not mindless of thy sire King Brute,
Who loved his loyal servants even as they
Loved him. Yea, surely, bitter were the fruit,
Prince Camber, and the tree rotten at root
That bare it, whence my tongue should take today
For thee the taste of poisonous treason.

CAMBER.

Nay,
What boots it though thou plight thy word to boot?
True servant wast thou to my sire King Brute,
And Brute thy king true master to thee.

DEBON.

Yea.
Troy, ere her towers dropped hurtling down in flame,
Bare not a son more noble than the sire
Whose son begat thy father. Shame it were
Beyond all record in the world of shame,
If they that hither bore in heart that fire
Which none save men of heavenly heart may bear

Had left no sign, though Troy were spoiled and sacked,
That heavenly was the seed they saved.

CAMBER.

No sign?
Though nought my fame be,--though no praise of mine
Be worth men's tongues for word or thought or act -
Shall fame forget my brother Albanact,
Or how those Huns who drank his blood for wine
Poured forth their own for offering to Locrine?
Though all the soundless maze of time were tracked,
No men should man find nobler.

DEBON.

Surely none.
No man loved ever more than I thy brothers,
Prince.

CAMBER.

Ay--for them thy love is bright like spring,
And colder toward me than the wintering sun.
What am I less--what less am I than others,
That thus thy tongue discrowns my name of king,
Dethrones my title, disanoints my state,
And pricks me down but petty prince?

DEBON.

My lord -

CAMBER.

Ay? must my name among their names stand scored
Who keep my brother's door or guard his gate?
A lordling--princeling--one that stands to wait -
That lights him back to bed or serves at board.
Old man, if yet thy foundering brain record
Aught--if thou know that once my sire was great,
Then must thou know he left no less to me,
His youngest, than to those my brethren born,
Kingship.

DEBON.

I know it. Your servant, sire, am I,
Who lived so long your sire's.

CAMBER.

And how had he
Endured thy silence or sustained thy scorn?
Why must I know not what thou knowest of?

DEBON.

Why?
Hast thou not heard, king, that a true man's trust
Is king for him of life and death? Locrine
Hath sealed with trust my lips--nay, prince, not mine -
His are they now.

CAMBER.

Thou art wise as he, and just,
And secret. God requite thee! yea, he must,
For man shall never. If my sword here shine
Sunward--God guard that reverend head of thine!

DEBON.

My blood should make thy sword the sooner rust,
And rot thy fame for ever. Strike.

CAMBER.

Thou knowest
I will not. Am I Scythian born, or Greek,
That I should take thy bloodshed on my hand?

DEBON.

Nay--if thou seest me soul to soul, and showest
Mercy -

CAMBER.

Thou think'st I would have slain thee? Speak.

DEBON.

Nay, then I will, for love of all this land:
Lest, if suspicion bring forth strife, and fear
Hatred, its face be withered with a curse;
Lest the eyeless doubt of unseen ill be worse

Than very truth of evil. Thou shalt hear
Such truth as falling in a base man's ear
Should bring forth evil indeed in hearts perverse;
But forth of thine shall truth, once known, disperse
Doubt: and dispersed, the cloud shall leave thee clear
In judgment--nor, being young, more merciless,
I think, than I toward hearts that erred and yearned,
Struck through with love and blind with fire of life
Enkindled. When the sharp and stormy stress
Of Scythian ravin round our borders burned
Eastward, and he that faced it first in strife,
King Albanact, thy brother, fought and fell,
Locrine our lord, and lordliest born of you, -
Thy chief, my prince, and mine--against them drew
With all the force our southern strengths might tell,
And by the strong mid water's seaward swell
That sunders half our Britain met and slew
The prince whose blood baptized its fame anew
And left no record of the name to dwell
Whereby men called it ere it wore his name,
Humber; and wide on wing the carnage went
Along the drenched red fields that felt the tramp
At once of fliers and slayers with feet like flame:
But the king halted, seeing a royal tent
Reared, with its ensign crowning all the camp,
And entered--where no Scythian spoil he found,
But one fair face, the Scythian's sometime prey,
A lady's whom their ships had borne away
By force of warlike hand from German ground,
A bride and queen by violent power fast bound
To the errant helmsman of their fierce array.
And her, left lordless by that ended fray,
Our lord beholding loved, and hailed, and crowned

Queen.

CAMBER.

Queen! and what perchance of Guendolen?
Slept she forsooth forgotten?

DEBON.

Nay, my lord
Knows that albeit their hands were precontract
By Brute your father dying, no man of men
May fasten hearts with hands in one accord.
The love our master knew not that he lacked
Fulfilled him even as heaven by dawn is filled
With fire and light that burns and blinds and leads
All men to wise or witless works or deeds,
Beholding, ere indeed he wist or willed,
Eyes that sent flame through veins that age had chilled.

CAMBER.

Thine--with that grey goat's fleece on chin, sir? Needs
Must she be fair: thou, wrapt in age's weeds,
Whose blood, if time have touched it not and stilled,
The sun's own fire must once have kindled,--thou
Sing praise of soft-lipped women? doth not shame
Sting thee, to sound this minstrel's note, and gild
A girl's proud face with praises, though her brow
Were bright as dawn's? And had her grace no name
For men to worship by? Her name?

DEBON.

Estrild.

CAMBER.

My brother is a prince of paramours -
Eyes coloured like the springtide sea, and hair
Bright as with fire of sundawn--face as fair
As mine is swart and worn with haggard hours,
Though less in years than his--such hap was ours
When chance drew forth for us the lots that were
Hid close in time's clenched hand: and now I swear,
Though his be goodlier than the stars or flowers,
I would not change this head of mine, or crown
Scarce worth a smile of his--thy lord Locrine's -
For that fair head and crown imperial; nay,
Not were I cast by force of fortune down
Lower than the lowest lean serf that prowls and pines
And loathes for fear all hours of night and day.

DEBON.

What says my lord? how means he?

CAMBER.

Vex not thou
Thine old hoar head with care to learn of me
This. Great is time, and what he wills to be
Is here or ever proof may bring it: now,
Now is the future present. If thy vow
Constrain thee not, yet would I know of thee

One thing: this lustrous love-bird, where is she?
What nest is hers on what green flowering bough
Deep in what wild sweet woodland?

DEBON.

Good my lord,
Have I not sinned already--flawed my faith,
To lend such ear even to such royal suit?

CAMBER.

Yea, by my kingdom hast thou--by my sword,
Yea. Now speak on.

DEBON.

Yet hope--or honour--saith
I did not ill to trust the blood of Brute
Within thee. Not prince Hector's sovereign soul,
The light of all thy lineage, more abhorred
Treason than all his days did Brute my lord.
My trust shall rest not in thee less than whole.

CAMBER.

Speak, then: too long thou falterest nigh the goal.

DEBON.

There is a bower built fast beside a ford
In Essex, held in sure and secret ward
Of woods and walls and waters, still and sole

As love could choose for harbourage: there the king
Keeps close from all men now these seven years since
The light wherein he lives: and there hath she
Borne him a maiden child more sweet than spring.

CAMBER.

A child her daughter? there now hidden?

DEBON.

Prince,
What ails thee?

CAMBER.

Nought. This river's name?

DEBON.

The Ley.

CAMBER.

Nigh Leytonstone in Essex--called of old
By men thine elders Durolitum? There
Are hind and fawn couched close in one green lair?
Speak: hast thou not my faith in pawn, to hold
Fast as my brother's heart this love, untold
And undivined of all men? must I swear
Twice--I, to thee?

DEBON.

But if thou set no snare,
Why shine thine eyes so sharp? I am overbold:
Sir, pardon me.

CAMBER.

My sword shall split thine heart
With pardon if thou palter with me.

DEBON.

Sir,
There is the place: but though thy brow be grim
As hell--I knew thee not the man thou art -
I will not bring thee to it.

CAMBER.

For love of her?
Nay--better shouldst thou know my love of him.
[Exeunt.

ACT II.

SCENE I.--The banks of the Ley.

Enter ESTRILD and SABRINA.

SABRINA.

But will my father come not? not today,
Mother?

ESTRILD.

God help thee! child, I cannot say.
Why this of all days yet in summer's sight?

SABRINA.

My birthday!

ESTRILD.

That should bring him--if it may.

SABRINA.

May should be must: he must not be away.
His faith was pledged to me as king and knight.

ESTRILD.

Small fear he should not keep it--if he might.

SABRINA.

Might! and a king's might his? do kings bear sway
For nought, that aught should keep him hence till night?
Why didst thou bid God help me when I sought
To know but of his coming?

ESTRILD.

Even for nought
But laughter even to think how strait a bound
Shuts in the measure of thy sight and thought
Who seest not why thy sire hath heed of aught
Save thee and me--nor wherefore men stand crowned
And girt about with empire.

SABRINA.

Have they found
Such joy therein as meaner things have wrought?
Sing me the song that ripples round and round.

ESTRILD (sings):-

Had I wist, quoth spring to the swallow,
That earth could forget me, kissed
By summer, and lured to follow
Down ways that I know not, I,
My heart should have waxed not high:
Mid March would have seen me die,
Had I wist.

Had I wist, O spring, said the swallow,
That hope was a sunlit mist
And the faint light heart of it hollow,
Thy woods had not heard me sing,
Thy winds had not known my wing;
It had faltered ere thine did, spring,
Had I wist.

SABRINA.

That song is hardly even as wise as I -
Nay, very foolishness it is. To die
In March before its life were well on wing,
Before its time and kindly season--why
Should spring be sad--before the swallows fly -
Enough to dream of such a wintry thing?
Such foolish words were more unmeet for spring
Than snow for summer when his heart is high;
And why should words be foolish when they sing?
The song-birds are not.

ESTRILD.

Dost thou understand,
Child, what the birds are singing?

SABRINA.

All the land
Knows that: the water tells it to the rushes
Aloud, and lower and softlier to the sand:
The flower-fays, lip to lip and hand in hand,
Laugh and repeat it all till darkness hushes
Their singing with a word that falls and crushes
All song to silence down the river-strand
And where the hawthorns hearken for the thrushes.
And all the secret sense is sweet and wise
That sings through all their singing, and replies
When we would know if heaven be gay or grey
And would not open all too soon our eyes
To look perchance on no such happy skies -
As sleep brings close and waking blows away.

ESTRILD.

What gives thy fancy faith enough to say
This?

SABRINA.

Why, meseems the sun would hardly rise
Else, nor the world be half so glad of day.

ESTRILD.

Why didst thou crave of me that song, Sabrina?

SABRINA.

Because, methought, though one were king or queen
And had the world to play with, if one missed
What most were good to have, such joy, I ween,
Were woful as a song with sobs between
And well might wail for ever, 'Had I wist!'
And might my father do but as he list,
And make this day what other days have been,
I should not shut tonight mine eyes unkissed.

ESTRILD.

I wis thou wouldst not.

SABRINA.

Then I would he were
No king at all, and save his golden hair
Wore on his gracious head no golden crown.
Must he be king for ever?

ESTRILD.

Not if prayer
Could lift from off his heart that crown of care
And draw him toward us as with music down.

SABRINA.

Not so, but upward to us. He would but frown
To hear thee talk as though the woodlands there
Were built no lordlier than the wide-walled town.
Thou knowest, when I desire of him to see
What manner of crown that wreath of towers may be
That makes its proud head shine like older Troy's,
His brows are bent even while he laughs on me
And bids me think no more thereon than he,
For flowers are serious things, but towers are toys.

ESTRILD.

Ay, child; his heart was less care's throne than joy's,
Power's less than love's friend ever: and with thee
His mood that plays is blither than a boy's.

SABRINA.

I would the boy would give the maid her will.

ESTRILD.

Has not thine heart as mine has here its fill?

SABRINA.

So have our hearts while sleeping--till they wake.

ESTRILD.

Too soon is this for waking: sleep thou still.

SABRINA.

Bid then the dawn sleep, and the world lie chill.

ESTRILD.

This nest is warm for one small wood-dove's sake.

SABRINA.

And warm the world that feels the sundawn break.

ESTRILD.

But hath my fledgeling cushat here slept ill?

SABRINA.

No plaint is this, but pleading, that I make.

ESTRILD.

Plead not against thine own glad life: the plea
Were like a wrangling babe's that fain would be
Free from the help its hardy heart contemns,
Free from the hand that guides and guards it, free
To take its way and sprawl and stumble. See!
Have we not here enough of diadems
Hung high round portals pillared smooth with stems
More fair than marble?

SABRINA.

This is but the Ley:
I fain would look upon the lordlier Thames.

ESTRILD.

A very water-bird thou art: the river
So draws thee to it that, seeing, my heart-strings quiver
And yearn with fear lest peril teach thee fear
Too late for help or daring to deliver.

SABRINA.

Nay, let the wind make willows weep and shiver:
Me shall nor wind nor water, while I hear
What goodly words saith each in other's ear.
And which is given the gift, and which the giver,
I know not, but they take and give good cheer.

ESTRILD.

Howe'er this be, thou hast no heed of mine,
To take so little of this life of thine
I gave and would not see thee cast away
For childishness in childhood, though it shine
For me sole comfort, for my lord Locrine
Chief comfort in the world.

SABRINA.

Nay, mother, nay,
Make me not weep with chiding: wilt thou say

I love thee not? Hark! see, my sire for sign!
I hear his horse.

ESTRILD.

He comes!

SABRINA.

He comes today!
[Exeunt

SCENE II.--Troynovant. A Room in the Palace.

Enter GUENDOLEN and CAMBER.

GUENDOLEN.

I know not, sir, what ails you to desire
Such audience of me as I give.

CAMBER.

What ails
Me, sister? Were the heart in me no higher
Than his who heeds no more than harpers' tales
Such griefs as set a sister's heart on fire -

GUENDOLEN.

Then were my brother now at rest in Wales,
And royal.

CAMBER.

Am I less than royal here?

GUENDOLEN.

Even here as there alike, sir.

CAMBER.

Dost thou fear
Nothing?

GUENDOLEN.

My princely cousin, not indeed
Much that might hap at word or will of thine.

CAMBER.

Ay--meanest am I of my father's seed,
If men misjudge not, cousin; and Locrine
Noblest.

GUENDOLEN.

Should I gainsay their general rede,
My heart would mock me.

CAMBER.

Such a spirit as mine
Being spiritless--my words heartless--mine acts
Faint shadows of Locrine's or Albanact's?

GUENDOLEN.

Nay--not so much--I said not so. Say thou
What thou wouldst have--if aught thou wouldst--with me.

CAMBER.

No man might see thine eyes and lips and brow
Who would not--what he durst not crave of thee.

GUENDOLEN.

Ay, verily? And thy spirit exalts thee now
So high that these thy words fly forth so free,
And fain thine act would follow--flying above
Shame's reach and fear's? What gift may this be? Love?
Or liking? or compassion?

CAMBER.

Take not thus
Mine innocent words amiss, nor wrest awry
Their piteous purpose toward thee.

GUENDOLEN.

Piteous!

Who lives so low and looks upon the sky
As would desire--who shares the sun with us
That might deserve thy pity?

CAMBER.

Thou.

GUENDOLEN.

Not I,
Though I were cast out hence, cast off, discrowned,
Abject, ungirt of all that guards me round,
Naked. What villainous madness, knave and king,
Is this that puts upon thy babbling tongue
Poison?

CAMBER.

The truth is as a snake to sting
That breathes ill news: but where its fang hath stung
The very pang bids health and healing spring.
God knows the grief wherewith my spirit is wrung -
The spirit of thee so scorned, so misesteemed,
So mocked with strange misprision and misdeemed
Merciless, false, unbrotherly--to take
Such task upon it as may burn thine heart
With bitterer hatred of me that I spake
What, had I held my peace and crept apart
And tamed my soul to silence for thy sake
And mercy toward the royal thing thou art,
Chance haply might have made a fiery sword
To slay thee with--slay thee, and spare thy lord.

GUENDOLEN.

Worse had it done to slay my lord, and spare
Me. Wilt thou now show mercy toward me? Then
Strike with that sword mine heart through--if thou dare.
All know thy tongue's edge deadly.

CAMBER.

Guendolen,
Thou seest me like a vassal bound to bear
All bitter words that bite the hearts of men
From thee, so be it this please thy wrath. I stand
Slave of thy tongue and subject of thine hand,
And pity thee. Take, if thou wilt, my head;
Give it my brother. Thou shalt hear me speak
First, though the soothfast word that hangs unsaid
As yet, being spoken,--albeit this hand be weak
And faint this heart, thou sayest--should strike thee dead
Even with that rose of wrath on brow and cheek.

GUENDOLEN.

I hold not thee too faint of heart to slay
Women. Say forth whate'er thou hast heart to say.

CAMBER.

Silence I have not heart to keep, and see
Scorn and derision gird thee round with shame,
Not knowing what all thy serfs who mock at thee
Know, and make mirth and havoc of thy name.
Does this not move thee?

GUENDOLEN.

How should aught move me
Fallen from such tongues as falsehood finds the same -
Such tongues as fraud or treasonous hate o'erscurfs
With leprous lust--a prince's or a serf's?

CAMBER.

That lust of the evil-speaking tongue which gives
Quick breath to deadly lies, and stings to life
The rottenness of falsehood, when it lives,
Falls dumb, and leaves the lie to bring forth strife.
The liar will say no more--his heart misgives
His knaveship--should he sunder man and wife?
Such, sister, in thy sight, it seems, am I.
Yet shalt thou take, to keep or cast it by,
The truth of shame I would not have thee hear, -
Not might I choose,--but choose I may not.

GUENDOLEN.

Shame
And truth? Shame never toward thine heart came near,
And all thy life hath hung about thy name.
Nor ever truth drew nigh the lips that fear
Whitens, and makes the blood that feeds them tame.
Speak all thou wilt--but even for shame, forsooth,
Talk not of shame--and tell me not of truth.

CAMBER.

Then shalt thou hear a lie. Thy loving lord

Loves none save thee; his heart's pulse beats in thine;
No fairer woman, captive of his sword,
Caught ever captive and subdued Locrine:
The god of lies bear witness. At the ford
Of Humber blood was never shed like wine:
Our brother Albanact lived, fought, and died,
Never: and I that swear it have not lied.

GUENDOLEN.

Fairer?

CAMBER.

They say it: but what are lies to thee?

GUENDOLEN.

Art thou nor man nor woman?

CAMBER.

Nay--I trust -
Man.

GUENDOLEN.

And hast heart to make thy spoil of me?

CAMBER.

Would God I might!

GUENDOLEN.

Thou art made of lies and lust -
Earth's worst is all too good for such to see,
And yet thine eyes turn heavenward--as they must,
Being man's--if man be such as thou--and soil
The light they see. Thou hast made of me thy spoil,
Thy scorn, thy profit--yea, my whole soul's plunder
Is all thy trophy, thy triumphal prize
And harvest reaped of thee; nay, trampled under
And rooted up and scattered. Yet the skies
That see thy trophies reared are full of thunder,
And heaven's high justice loves not lust and lies.

CAMBER.

Ill then should fare thy lord--if heaven be just,
And lies be lies, and lawless love be lust.

GUENDOLEN.

Thou liest. I know my lord and thee. Thou liest.

CAMBER.

If he be true and truth be false, I lie.

GUENDOLEN.

Thou art lowest of all men born--while he sits highest.

CAMBER.

Ay--while he sits. How long shall he sit high?

GUENDOLEN.

If I but whisper him of thee, thou diest.

CAMBER.

I fear not, if till then secure am I.

GUENDOLEN.

Secure as fools are hardy live thou still.

CAMBER.

While ill with good is guerdoned, good with ill.

GUENDOLEN.

I have it in my mind to take thine head.
Dost thou not fear to put me thus in fear?

CAMBER.

I fear nor man nor woman, quick nor dead:
And dead in spirit already stand'st thou here.

GUENDOLEN.

Thou darest not swear my lord hath wronged my bed.

Thou darest but smile and mutter, lie and leer.

CAMBER.

I swear no queen bore ever crown on brow
Who meeklier bore a heavier wrong than thou.

GUENDOLEN.

From thee will I bear nothing. Get thee hence:
Thine eyes defile me. Get thee from my sight.

CAMBER.

The gods defend thee, soul and spirit and sense,
From sense of things thou darest not read aright!
Farewell. [Exit.

GUENDOLEN.

Fare thou not well, and be defence
Far from thy soul cast naked forth by night!
Hate rose from hell a liar: love came divine
From heaven: yet she that bore thee bore Locrine.
[Exit.

ACT III.

SCENE I.--Troynovant. A Room in the Palace.

Enter LOCRINE and DEBON.

LOCRINE.

Thou knowest not what she knows or dreams of? why
Her face is dark and wan, her lip and eye
Restless and red as fever? Hast thou kept
Faith?

DEBON.

Has my master found my faith a lie
Once all these years through? have I strayed or slept
Once, when he bade me watch? what proof has leapt
At last to light against me?

LOCRINE.

Surely, none.
Weep not.

DEBON.

My lord's grey vassal hath not wept
Once, even since darkness covered from the sun
The woman's face--the sole sweet wifelike one -
Whose memory holds his heart yet fast: but now
Tears, were old age not poor in tears, might run
Free as the words that bid his stricken brow
Burn and bow down to hear them.

LOCRINE.

Hast not thou
Held counsel--played the talebearer whose tales
Bear plague abroad and poison, knowing not how -
Not with my wife nor brother?

DEBON.

Nought avails
Falsehood: and truth it is, the king of Wales
So plied me, sir, with force of craft and threat -

LOCRINE.

That thou, whose faith swerves never, flags nor fails
Nor falters, being as stars are loyal, yet
Wast found as those that fall from heaven, forget
Their station, shoot and shudder down to death
Deep as the pit of hell? What snares were set
To take thy soul--what mist of treasonous breath
Made blind in thee the sense that quickeneth
In true men's inward eyesight, when they know

And know not how they know the word it saith,
The warning word that whispers loud or low -
I ask not: be it enough these things are so.
Thou hast played me false.

DEBON.

Nay, now this long time since
We have seen the queen's face wan with wrath and woe -
Have seen her lip writhe and her eyelid wince
To take men's homage--proof that might convince
Of grief inexpiable and insatiate shame
Her spirit in all men's judgment.

LOCRINE.

But the prince -
My brother, whom thou knowest by proof, not fame,
A coward whose heart is all a flickering flame
That fain would burn and dares not--whence had he
The poison that he gave her? Speak: this came
By chance--mishap--most haplessly for thee
Who hadst my heart in thine, and madest of me
No more than might for folly's sake or fear's
Be bared for even such eyes as his to see?
Old friend that wast, I would not see thy tears.
God comfort thy dishonour!

DEBON.

All these years
Have I not served thee?

LOCRINE.

Yea. So cheer thee now.

DEBON.

Cheered be the traitor, whom the true man cheers?
Nay, smite me: God can be not such as thou,
And will not damn me with forgiveness. How
Hast thou such heart, to comfort such as me?
God's thunder were less fearful than the brow
That frowns not on thy friend found false to thee.
Thy friend--thou said'st--thy friend. Strange friends are we.
Nay, slay me then--nay, slay me rather.

LOCRINE.

Friend,
Take comfort. God's wide-reaching will shall be
Here as of old accomplished, though it blend
All good with ill that none may mar or mend.
Thy works and mine are ripples on the sea.
Take heart, I say: we know not yet their end.
[Exeunt.

SCENE II.--Gardens of the Palace.

Enter CAMBER and MADAN.

CAMBER.

Hath no man seen thee?

MADAN.

Had he seen, and spoken,
His head should lose its tongue. I am far away
In Cornwall.

CAMBER.

Where the front of war is broken
By the onset of thy force--the rebel fray
Shattered. Had no man--canst thou surely say? -
Knowledge betimes, to give us knowledge here -
Us babblers, tongues made quick with fraud and fear -
That thou wast bound from Cornwall hither?

MADAN.

None,
I think, who knowing of steel and fire and cord
That they can smite and burn and strangle one
Would loose without leave of his parting lord
The tongue that else were sharper than a sword
To cut the throat it sprang from.

CAMBER.

Nephew mine,
I have ever loved thee--not thy sire Locrine
More--and for very and only love of thee
Have I desired, or ever even thy mother
Beheld thee, here to know of thee and me
Which loves her best--her and thy sire my brother.

MADAN.

He being away, far hence--and so none other -
Not he--should share the knowledge?

CAMBER.

Surely not
He. Knowest thou whither hence he went?

MADAN.

God wot,
No: haply toward some hidden paramour.

CAMBER.

And that should set not, for thy mother's sake,
And thine, the heart in thee on fire?

MADAN.

An hour
Is less than even the time wherein we take

Breath to let loose the word that fain would break,
And cannot, even for passion,--if we set
An hour against the length of life: and yet
Less in account of life should be those hours -
Should be? should be not, live not, be not known,
Not thought of, not remembered even as ours, -
Whereon the flesh or fancy bears alone
Rule that the soul repudiates for its own,
Rejects and mocks and mourns for, and reclaims
Its nature, none the ignobler for the shames
That were but shadows on it--shed but shade
And perished. If thy brother and king, my sire -

CAMBER.

No king of mine is he--we are equal, weighed
Aright in state, though here his throne stand higher.

MADAN.

So be it. I say, if even some earth-born fire
Have ever lured the loftiest head that earth
Sees royal, toward a charm of baser birth
And force less godlike than the sacred spell
That links with him my mother, what were this
To her or me?

CAMBER.

To her no more than hell
To souls cast forth who hear all hell-fire hiss
All round them, and who feel the red worm's kiss
Shoot mortal poison through the heart that rests

Immortal: serpents suckled at her breasts,
Fire feeding on her limbs, less pain should be
Than sense of pride laid waste and love laid low,
If she be queen or woman: and to thee -

MADAN.

To me that wax not woman though I know
This, what shall hap or hap not?

CAMBER.

Were it so,
It should not irk thee, she being wronged alone;
Thy mother's bed, and not thy father's throne,
Being soiled with usurpation. Ay? but say
That now mine uncle and her sire lies dead
And helpless now to help her, or affray
The heart wherein her ruin and thine were bred,
Not she were cast forth only from his bed,
But thou, loathed issue of a contract loathed
Since first their hands were joined not but betrothed,
Wert cast forth out of kingship? stripped of state,
Unmade his son, unseated, unallowed,
Discrowned, disorbed, discrested--thou, but late
Prince, and of all men's throats acclaimed aloud,
Of all men's hearts accepted and avowed
Prince, now proclaimed for some sweet bastard's sake
Peasant?

MADAN.

Thy sire was sure less man than snake,

Though mine miscall thee brother.

CAMBER.

Coward or mad?
Which might one call thee rather, whose harsh heart
Envenoms so thy tongue toward one that had
No thought less kindly--toward even thee that art
Kindless--than best beseems a kinsman's part?

MADAN.

Lay not on me thine own foul shame, whose tongue
Would turn my blood to poison, while it stung
Thy brother's fame to death. I know my sire
As shame knows thee--and better no man knows
Aught.

CAMBER.

Have thy will, then: take thy full desire:
Drink dry the draught of ruin: bid all blows
Welcome: being harsh with friends, be mild with foes,
And give shame thanks for buffets. Yet I thought -
But how should help avail where heart is nought?

MADAN.

Yet--thou didst think to help me?

CAMBER.

Kinsman, ay.

My hand had held the field beside thine own,
And all wild hills that know my rallying cry
Had poured forth war for heart's pure love alone
To help thee--wouldst thou heed me--to thy throne.

MADAN.

For pure heart's love? what wage holds love in fee?
Might half my kingdom serve? Nay, mock not me,
Fair uncle: should I cleave the crown in twain
And gird thy temples with the goodlier half,
Think'st thou my debt might so be paid again -
Thy sceptre made a more imperial staff
Than sways as now thy hill-folk?

CAMBER.

Dost thou laugh?
Were this too much for kings to give and take?
If warrior Wales do battle for thy sake,
Should I that kept thy crown for thee be held
Worth less than royal guerdon?

MADAN.

Keep thine own,
And let the loud fierce knaves thy brethren quelled
Ward off the wolves whose hides should line thy throne,
Wert thou no coward, no recreant to the bone,
No liar in spirit and soul and heartless heart,
No slave, no traitor--nought of all thou art.
A thing like thee, made big with braggart breath,
Whose tongue shoots fire, whose promise poisons trust,

Would cast a shieldless soldier forth to death
And wreck three realms to sate his rancorous lust
With ruin of them who have weighed and found him dust.
Get thee to Wales: there strut in speech and swell:
And thence betimes God speed thee safe to hell.
[Exeunt severally.

ACT IV.

SCENE I.--The banks of the Ley.

Enter LOCRINE and ESTRILD.

LOCRINE.

If thou didst ever love me, love me now.
I am weary at heart of all on earth save thee.
And yet I lie: and yet I lie not. Thou -
Dost thou not think for love's sake scorn of me?

ESTRILD.

As earth of heaven: as morning of the sun.

LOCRINE.

Nay, what thinks evening, whom he leaves undone?

ESTRILD.

Thou madest me queen and woman: though my life
Were taken, these thou couldst not take again,

The gifts thou gavest me. More am I than wife,
Whom, till my tyrant by thy strength were slain
And by thy love my servile shame cast out,
My naked sorrows clothed and girt about
With princelier pride than binds the brows of queens,
Thou sawest of all things least and lowest alive.
What means thy doubt?

LOCRINE.

Fear knows not what it means:
And I was fearful even of clouds that drive
Across the dawn, and die--of all, of nought -
Winds whispering on the darkling ways of thought,
Sunbeams that flash like fire, and hopes like fears
That slay themselves, and live again, and die.
But in mine eyes thy light is, in mine ears
Thy music: I am thine, and more than I,
Being half of thy sweet soul.

ESTRILD.

Woe worth me then!
For one requires thee wholly.

LOCRINE.

Guendolen?

ESTRILD.

I said she was the fairer--and I lied not.

LOCRINE.

Thou art the fairest fool alive.

ESTRILD.

But she,
Being wise, exceeds me: yet, so she divide not
Thine heart, my best-beloved of liars, with me,
I care not--nor I will not care. Some part
She hath had, it may be, of thy fond false heart -
Nay, couldst thou choose? but now, though she be fairer,
Let her take all or none: I will not be
Partaker of her perfect sway, nor sharer
With any on earth more dear or less to thee.
Nay, be not wroth: what wilt thou have me say?
That I can love thee less than she can? Nay,
Thou knowest I will not ill to her; but she -
Would she not burn my child and me with fire
To wreak herself, who loved thee once, on thee?

LOCRINE.

Thy fear is darker, child, than her desire.

ESTRILD.

I fear not her at all: I would not fear
The one thing fearful to me yet, who here
Sit walled around with waters and with woods
From all things fearful but the fear of change.

LOCRINE.

Fear thou not that: for nothing born eludes
Time; and the joy were sorrowful and strange
That should endure for ever. Yea, I think
Such joy would pray for sorrow's cup to drink,
Such constancy desire an end, for mere
Long weariness of watching. Thou and I
Have all our will of life and loving here, -
A heavenlier heaven on earth: but we shall die,
And if we died not, love we might outlive
As now shall love outlive us.

ESTRILD.

We?

LOCRINE.

Forgive!

ESTRILD.

King! and I held thee more than man!

LOCRINE.

God wot,
Thou art more than I--more strong and wise;
I know
Thou couldst not live one hour if love were not.

ESTRILD

And thou? -

LOCRINE.

I would not. All the world were woe,
And all the day night, if the love I bear thee
Were plucked out of the life wherein I wear thee
As crown and comfort of its nights and days.

ESTRILD.

Thou liest--for love's sake and for mine--and I
Lie not, who swear by thee whereon I gaze
I hold no truth so hallowed as the lie
Wherewith my love redeems me from the snare
Dark doubt had set to take me.

LOCRINE.

Wilt thou swear
- By what thou wilt soever--by the sun
That sees us--by the light of all these flowers -
By this full stream whose waves we hear not run -
By all that is nor mine nor thine, but ours -
That thou didst ever doubt indeed? or dream
That doubt, whose breath bids love of love misdeem,
Were other than the child of hate and hell,
The liar first-born of falsehood?

ESTRILD.

Nay--I think -
God help me!--hardly. Never? can I tell?
When half our soul and all our senses sink
From dream to dream down deathward, slain with sleep,
How may faith hold assurance fast, or keep
Her power to cast out fear for love's sake?

LOCRINE.

Could doubt not thee, waking or sleeping.

ESTRILD.

No -
Thou art not mad. How should the sunlit sky
Betray the sun? cast out the sunshine? So
Art thou to me as light to heaven: should light
Die, were not heaven as hell and noon as night?
And wherefore should I hold more dear than life
Death? Could I live, and lack thee? Thou, O king,
Hast lands and lordships--and a royal wife -
And rule of seas that tire the seamew's wing -
And fame as far as fame can travel; I,
What have I save this home wherein to die,
Except thou love me? Nay, nor home were this,
No place to die or live in, were I sure
Thou didst not love me. Swear not by this kiss
That love lives longer--faith may more endure -
Than one poor kiss that passes with the breath
Of lips that gave it life at once and death.
Why shouldst thou swear, and wherefore should I trust?

When day shall drive not night from heaven, and night
Shall chase not day to deathward, then shall dust
Be constant--and the stars endure the sight
Of dawn that shall not slay them.

LOCRINE.

By thine eyes
- Turned stormier now than stars in bare-blown skies
Wherethrough the wind rings menace,--I will swear
Nought: so shall fear, mistrust, and jealous hate
Lie foodless, if not fangless. Thou, so fair
That heaven might change for thee the seal of fate,
How darest thou doubt thy power on souls of men?

ESTRILD.

What vows were those that won thee Guendolen?

LOCRINE.

I sware not so to her. Thou knowest -

ESTRILD.

Not I.
Thou knowest that I know nothing.

LOCRINE.

Nay, I know
That nothing lives under the sweet blue sky
Worth thy sweet heeding, wouldst thou think but so,

Save love--wherewith thou seest thy world fulfilled.

ESTRILD.

Ay,--would I see but with thine eyes.

LOCRINE.

Estrild,
Estrild!

ESTRILD.

No soft reiterance of my name
Can sing my sorrow down that comes and goes
And colours hope with fear and love with shame.
Rose hast thou called me: were I like the rose,
Happier were I than woman: she survives
Not by one hour, like us of longer lives,
The sun she lives in and the love he gives
And takes away: but we, when love grows sere,
Live yet, while trust in love no longer lives,
Nor drink for comfort with the dying year
Death.

LOCRINE.

Wouldst thou drink forgetfulness for wine
To heal thine heart of love toward me?

ESTRILD.

Locrine,

Locrine!

LOCRINE.

Thou wouldst not: do not mock me then,
Saying out of evil heart, in evil jest,
Thy trust is dead to meward.

ESTRILD.

King of men,
Wouldst thou, being only of all men lordliest,
Be lord of women's thoughts and loving fears?
Nay, wert thou less than lord of worlds and years,
Of stars and suns and seasons, couldst thou dream
To take such empire on thee?

LOCRINE.

Nay, not I -
No more than she there playing beside the stream
To slip within a stormier stream and die.

ESTRILD.

She runs too near the brink. Sabrina!

LOCRINE.

See,
Her hands are lily-laden: let them be
A flower-sweet symbol for us.
Enter SABRINA.

SABRINA.

Sire! O sire,
See what fresh flowers--you knew not these before -
The spring has brought, to serve my heart's desire,
Forth of the river's barren bed! no more
Will I rebuke these banks for sterile sloth
When spring restores the woodlands. By my troth,
I hoped not, when you came again, to bring
So large a tribute worth so full a smile.

LOCRINE.

Child! how should I to thee pay tribute?

ESTRILD.

King,
Thou hast not kissed her.

LOCRINE.

Dare my lips defile
Heaven? O my love, in sight of her and thee
I marvel how the sun should look on me
And spare to turn his beams to fire.

ESTRILD.

The child
Hears, and is troubled.

SABRINA.

Did I wrong, to say
'Sire?' but you bade me say so. He is mild,
And will not chide me. Father!

ESTRILD.

Hear'st thou?

LOCRINE.

Yea -
I hear. I would the world beyond our sight
Were dead as worlds forgotten.

ESTRILD.

Wouldst thou fright
Her?

LOCRINE.

Hath all sense forsaken me? Sabrina,
Thou dost not fear me?

SABRINA.

No. But when your eyes
Wax red and dark, with flaughts of fire between,
I fear them--or they fright me.

LOCRINE.

Wert thou wise,
They would not. Never have I looked on thee
So.

SABRINA.

Nay--I fear not what might fall on me.
Here laughs my father--here my mother smiles -
Here smiles and laughs the water--what should I
Fear?

LOCRINE.

Nought more fearful than the water's wiles -
Which whoso fears not ere he fear shall die.

SABRINA.

Die? and is death no less an ill than dread?
I had liefer die than be nor quick nor dead.
I think there is no death but fear of death.

LOCRINE.

Of death or life or anything but love
What knowest thou?

SABRINA.

Less than these, my mother saith -
Less than the flowers that seeing all heaven above

Fade and wax hoar or darken, lose their trust
And leave their joy and let their glories rust
And die for fear ere winter wound them: we
Live no less glad of snowtime than of spring:
It cannot change my father's face for me
Nor turn from mine away my mother's. King
They call thee: hath thy kingship made thee less
In height of heart than we are?

LOCRINE.

No, and yes.
Here sits my heart at height of hers and thine,
Laughing for love: here not the quiring birds
Sing higher than sings my spirit: I am here Locrine,
Whom no sound vexes here of swords or words,
No cloud of thought or thunder: were my life
Crowned but as lord and sire of child and wife,
Throned but as prince of woodland, bank and bower,
My joys were then imperial, and my state
Firm as a star, that now is as a flower.

SABRINA.

Thou shouldst not then--if joy grow here so great -
Part from us.

LOCRINE.

No: for joy grows elsewhere scant.

SABRINA.

I would fain see the towers of Troynovant.

LOCRINE.

God keep thine eyes fulfilled with sweeter sights,
And this one from them ever!

SABRINA.

Why? Men say
Thine halls are full of guests, princes and knights,
And lordly musters of superb array;
Why are we thence alone, and alway?

ESTRILD.

Peace,
Child: let thy babble change its note, or cease
Here; is thy sire not wiser--by God's grace -
Than I or thou?

LOCRINE.

Wouldst thou too see fulfilled
The fear whose shadow fallen on joy's fair face
Strikes it more sad than sorrow's own? Estrild,
Wast thou then happier ere this wildwood shrine
Hid thee from homage, left thee but Locrine
For worshipper less worthy grace of thee
Than those thy sometime suppliants?

ESTRILD.

Nay; my lord
Takes too much thought--if tongues ring true--for me.

LOCRINE.

Such tongues ring falser than a broken chord
Whose jar distunes the music.

ESTRILD.

Wilt thou stay
But three nights here?

LOCRINE.

I had need be hence today.

ESTRILD.

Go.

SABRINA.

But I bid thee tarry; what am I
That thou shouldst heed not what I bid thee?

LOCRINE.

Queen
And empress more imperious and more high
And regent royaller than time hath seen

And mightier mistress of thy sire and thrall:
Yet must I go. But ere the next moon fall
Again will I grow happy.

ESTRILD.

Who can say?

LOCRINE.

So much can I--except the stars combine
Unseasonably to stay me.

ESTRILD.

Let them stay
The tides, the seasons rather. Love! Locrine!
I never parted from thee, nor shall part,
Save with a fire more keen than fire at heart:
But now the pang that wrings me, soul and sense,
And turns fair day to darkness deep as hell,
Warns me, the word that seals thy parting hence -
'Farewell'--shall bid us never more fare well.

SABRINA.

Lo! she too bids thee tarry; dost thou not
Hear?

LOCRINE.

Might I choose, small need were hers, God wot,
Or thine, to bid me tarry. When I come

Again -

SABRINA.

Thou shalt not see me: I will hide
From sight of such a sire--or bow down dumb
Before him--strong and hard as he in pride -
And so thou shalt not hear me.

LOCRINE.

Who can tell?
So now say I.

ESTRILD.

God keep my lord!

LOCRINE.

Farewell.
[Exeunt.

SCENE II.--Troynovant. A Room in the Palace.

Enter GUENDOLEN and MADAN.

GUENDOLEN.

Come close, and look upon me. Child or man, -
I know not how to call thee, being my child,
Who know not how myself am called, nor can -
God witness--tell thee what should she be styled
Who bears the brand and burden set on her
That man hath set on me--the lands are wild
Whence late I bade thee hither, swift of spur
As he that rides to guard his mother's life;
Thou hast found nought loathlier there, nought hate-fuller
In all the wilds that seethe with fluctuant strife,
Than here besets thine advent. Son, if thou
Be son of mine, and I thy father's wife -

MADAN.

If heaven be heaven, and God be God.

GUENDOLEN.

As now
We know not if they be. Give me thine hand.
Thou hast mine eyes beneath thy father's brow, -
And therefore bears it not the traitor's brand.
Swear--But I would not bid thee swear in vain
Nor bind thee ere thine own soul understand,

Ere thine own heart be molten with my pain,
To do such work for bitter love of me
As haply, knowing my heart, thou wert not fain -
Even thou--to take upon thee--bind on thee -
Set all thy soul to do or die.

MADAN.

I swear.

GUENDOLEN.

And though thou sworest not, yet the thing should be.
The burden found for me so sore to bear
Why should I lay on any hand but mine,
Or bid thine own take part therein, and wear
A father's blood upon it--here--for sign?
Ay, now thou pluck'st it forth of hers to whom
Thou sworest and gavest it plighted. O Locrine,
Thy seed it was that sprang within my womb,
Thine, and none other--traitor born and liar,
False-faced, false-tongued--the fire of hell consume
Me, thee, and him for ever!

MADAN.

Hath my sire
Wronged thee?

GUENDOLEN.

Thy sire? my lord? the flower of men?
How?

MADAN.

For thy tongue was tipped but now with fire -
With fire of hell--against him.

GUENDOLEN.

Now, and then,
Are twain; thou knowest not women, how their tongue
Takes fire, and straight learns patience: Guendolen
Is there no more than crownless woman, wrung
At heart with anguish, and in utterance mad
As even the meanest whom a snake hath stung
So near the heart that all the pulse it had
Grows palpitating poison. Wilt thou know
Whence?

MADAN.

Could I heal it, then mine own were glad.

GUENDOLEN.

What think'st thou were the bitterest wrong, the woe
Least bearable by woman, worst of all
That man might lay upon her? Nay, thou art slow:
Speak: though thou speak but folly. Silent? Call
To mind whatso thou hast ever heard of ill
Most monstrous, that should turn to fire and gall
The milk and blood of maid or mother--still
Thou shalt not find, I think, what he hath done -
What I endure, and die not. For my will
It is that holds me yet alive, O son,

Till all my wrong be wroken, here to keep
Fast watch, a living soul before the sun,
Anhungered and athirst for night and sleep,
That will not slake the ravin of her thirst
Nor quench her fire of hunger, till she reap
The harvest loved of all men, last as first -
Vengeance.

MADAN.

What wrong is this he hath done thee? Words
Are edgeless weapons: live we blest or curst,
No jot the more of evil or good engirds
The life with bitterest curses compassed round
Or girt about with blessing. Hinds and herds
Wage threats and brawl and wrangle: wind and sound
Suffice their souls for vengeance: we require
Deeds, and till place for these and time be found
Silence. What bids thee bid me slay my sire?

GUENDOLEN.

I praise the gods that gave me thee: thine heart
Is none of his, no changeling's in desire,
No coward's as who begat thee: mine thou art
All, and mine only. Lend me now thine ear:
Thou knowest -

MADAN.

What anguish holds thy lips apart
And strikes thee silent? Am I bound to hear
What thou to speak art bound not?

GUENDOLEN.

How my lord,
Our lord, thy sire--the king whose throne is here
Imperial--smote and drove the wolf-like horde
That raged against us from the raging east,
And how their chief sank in the unsounded ford
He thought to traverse, till the floods increased
Against him, and he perished: and Locrine
Found in his camp for sovereign spoil to feast
The sense of power with lustier joy than wine
A woman--Dost thou mock me?

MADAN.

And a fair
Woman, if all men lie not, mother mine -
I have heard so much. And then?

GUENDOLEN.

Thou dost not dare
Mock me?

MADAN.

I know not what should make thee mad
Though this and worse, howbeit it irk thee, were.
Art thou discrowned, dethroned, disrobed, unclad
Of empire? art thou powerless, bloodless, old?
This were some hurt: but now--thou shouldst be glad
To take this chance upon thee, and to hold
So large a lordly happiness in hand

As when my father's and thy lord's is cold
Shall leave in thine the sway of all this land.

GUENDOLEN.

And thou? no she-wolf whelps upon the wold
Whose brood is like thy mother's.

MADAN.

Nay--I stand
A man thy son before thee.

GUENDOLEN.

And a bold
Man: is thine heart flesh, or a burning brand
Lit to burn up and turn for thee to gold
The kingship of thy sire?

MADAN.

Why, blessed or banned,
We thrive alike--thou knowest it--why, but now
I said so,--scarce the glass has dropped one sand -
And thou didst smile on me--and all thy brow
Smiled.

GUENDOLEN.

Thou dost love then, thou, thy mother yet -
Me, dost thou love a little? None but thou
There is to love me; for the gods forget -

Nor shall one hear of me a prayer again;
Yea, none of all whose thrones in heaven are set
Shall hear, nor one of all the sons of men.

MADAN.

What wouldst thou have?

GUENDOLEN.

Thou knowest.

MADAN.

I know not. Speak.

GUENDOLEN.

Have I kept silence all this while?

MADAN.

What then?
What boots it though thy word, thine eye, thy cheek,
Seem all one fire together, if that fire
Sink, and thy face change, and thine heart wax weak,
To hear what deed should slake thy sore desire
And satiate thee with healing? This alone -
Except thine heart be softer toward my sire
Still than a maid's who hears a wood-dove moan
And weeps for pity--this should comfort thee:
His death.

GUENDOLEN.

And sight of Madan on his throne?

MADAN

What ailed thy wits, mother, to send for me?

GUENDOLEN.

Yet shalt thou not go back.

MADAN.

Why, what should I
Do here, where vengeance has not heart to be
And wrath dies out in weeping? Let it die -
And let me go.

GUENDOLEN.

I did not bid thee spare.

MADAN.

Speak then, and bid me smite.

GUENDOLEN.

Thy father?

MADAN.

Ay -
If thus it please my mother.

GUENDOLEN.

Dost thou dare
This?

MADAN.

Nay, I lust not after empire so
That for mine own hand I should haply care
To take this deed upon it: but the blow,
Thou sayest, that speeds my father forth of life,
Speeds too my mother forth of living woe
That till he dies may die not. If his wife
Set in his son's right hand the sword to slay -
No poison brewed of hell, no treasonous knife -
The sword that walks and shines and smites by day,
Not on his hand who takes the sword shall cleave
The blood that clings on hers who gives it.

GUENDOLEN.

Yea -
So be it. What levies wilt thou raise, to heave
Thy father from his seat?

MADAN.

Let that be nought

Of all thy care: do thou but trust--believe
Thy son's right hand no feebler than thy thought,
If that be strong to smite--and thou shalt see
Vengeance.

GUENDOLEN.

I will. But were thy musters brought
Whence now thou art come to cheer me, this should be
A sign for us of comfort.

MADAN.

Dost thou fear
Signs?

GUENDOLEN.

Nay, child, nay--thou art harsh as heaven to me -
I would but have of thee a word of cheer.

MADAN.

I am weak in words: my tongue can match not thine,
Mother.
Voices within] The king!

GUENDOLEN.

Hearst thou?
Voices within.] The king!

MADAN.

I hear.

Enter LOCRINE.

LOCRINE.

How fares my queen?

GUENDOLEN.

Well. And this child of mine -
How he may fare concerns not thee to know?

LOCRINE.

Why, well I see my boy fares well.

GUENDOLEN.

Locrine,
Thou art welcome as the sun to fields of snow.

LOCRINE.

But hardly would they hail the sun whose face
Dissolves them deathward. Was thy meaning so?

GUENDOLEN.

Make answer for me, Madan.

LOCRINE.

In thy place?
The boy's is not beside thee.

GUENDOLEN.

Speak, I say.

MADAN.

God guard my lord and father with his grace!

LOCRINE.

Well prayed, my child.

GUENDOLEN.

Children--who can but pray -
Pray better, if my sense not err, than we.
The God whom all the gods of heaven obey
Should hear them rather, seeing--as gods may see -
How pure of purpose is their perfect prayer.

LOCRINE.

I think not else--the better then for me.
But ours--what manner of child is this? the hair
Buds flowerwise round his darkening lips and chin,
This hand's young hardening palm knows how to bear
The sword-hilt's poise that late I laid therein -
Ha? doth not it?

GUENDOLEN.

Thine enemies know that well.

MADAN.

I make no boast of battles that have been;
But, so God help me, days unborn shall tell
What manner of heart my father gave me.

LOCRINE.

Good.
I doubt thee not.

GUENDOLEN.

In Cornwall they that fell
So found it, that of all their large-limbed brood
No bulk is left to brave thee.

LOCRINE.

Yea, I know
Our son hath given the wolf our foes for food
And won him worthy praise from friend or foe;
And heartier praise and trustier thanks from none,
Boy, than thy father pays thee.

GUENDOLEN.

Wouldst thou show
Thy love, thy thanks, thy fatherhood in one,

Thy perfect honour--yea, thy right to stand
Crowned, and lift up thine eyes against the sun
As one so pure in heart, so clean of hand,
So loyal and so royal, none might cast
A word against thee burning like a brand,
A sound that withers honour, and makes fast
The bondage of a recreant soul to shame -
Thou shouldst, or ever an hour be overpast,
Slay him.

LOCRINE.

Thou art mad.

GUENDOLEN.

What, is not then thy name
Locrine? and hath this boy done ill to thee?
Hath he not won him for thy love's sake fame?
Hath he not served thee loyally? is he
So much thy son, so little son of mine,
That men might call him traitor? May they see
The brand across his brow that reddens thine?
How shouldst thou dare--how dream--to let him live?
Is he not loyal? art not thou Locrine?
What less than death for guerdon shouldst thou give
My son who hath done thee service? Me thou hast given -
Who hast found me truer than falsehood can forgive -
Shame for my guerdon: yea, my heart is riven
With shame that once I loved thee.

LOCRINE.

Guendolen,
A woman's wrath should rest not unforgiven
Save of the slightest of the sons of men:
And no such slight and shameful thing am I
As would not yield thee pardon.

GUENDOLEN.

Slay me then.

LOCRINE.

Thee, or thy son? but now thou bad'st him die.

GUENDOLEN.

Thou liest: I bade thee slay him.

LOCRINE.

Art thou mad
Indeed?

GUENDOLEN.

O liar, is all the world a lie?
I bade thee, knowing thee what thou art--I bade
My lord and king and traitor slay my son -
A heartless hand that lacks the power it had
Smite one whose stroke shall leave it strengthless--one
Whose loyal loathing of his shame in thee

Shall cast it out of eyeshot of the sun.

LOCRINE.

Thou bad'st me slay him that he might--he, slay me?

GUENDOLEN.

Thou hast said--and yet thou hast lied not.

LOCRINE.

Hell's own hate
Brought never forth such fruit as thine.

GUENDOLEN.

But he
Is the issue of thy love and mine, by fate
Made one to no good issue. Didst thou trust
That grief should give to men disconsolate
Comfort, and treason bring forth truth, and dust
Blossom? What love, what reverence, what regard,
Shouldst thou desire, if God or man be just,
Of this thy son, or me more evil-starred,
Whom scorn salutes his mother?

LOCRINE.

How should scorn
Draw near thee, girt about with power for guard,
Power and good fame? unless reproach be born
Of these thy violent vanities of mood

That fight against thine honour.

GUENDOLEN.

Dost thou mourn
For that? Too careful art thou for my good,
Too tender and too true to me and mine,
For shame to make my heart or thine his food
Or scorn lay hold upon my fame or thine.
Art thou not pure as honour's perfect heart -
Not treason-cankered like my lord Locrine,
Whose likeness shows thee fairer than thou art
And falser than thy loving care of me
Would bid my faith believe thee?

LOCRINE.

What strange part
Is this that changing passion plays in thee?
Know'st thou me not?

GUENDOLEN.

Yea--witness heaven and hell,
And all the lights that lighten earth and sea,
And all that wrings my heart, I know thee well.
How should I love and hate and know thee not?

LOCRINE.

Thy voice is as the sound of dead love's knell.

GUENDOLEN.

Long since my heart has tolled it--and forgot
All save the cause that bade the death-bell sound
And cease and bring forth silence.

LOCRINE.

Is thy lot
Less fair and royal, girt with power and crowned, -
Than might fulfil the loftiest heart's desire?

GUENDOLEN.

Not air but fire it is that rings me round -
Thy voice makes all my brain a wheel of fire.
Man, what have I to do with pride of power?
Such pride perchance it was that moved my sire
To bid me wed--woe worth the woful hour! -
His brother's son, the brother's born above
Him as above me thou, the crown and flower
Of Britain, gentler-hearted than the dove
And mightier than the sunward eagle's wing:
But nought moved me save one thing only--love.

LOCRINE.

I know it.

GUENDOLEN.

Thou knowest? but this thou knowest not, king,
How near of kin are bitter love and hate -

Nor which of these may be the deadlier thing.

LOCRINE.

What wouldst thou?

GUENDOLEN.

Death. Would God my heart were great!
Then would I slay myself.

LOCRINE.

I dare not fear
That heaven hath marked for thee no fairer fate.

GUENDOLEN.

Ay! wilt thou slay me then--and slay me here?

LOCRINE.

Mock not thy wrath and me. No hair of thine
Would I--thou knowest it--hurt; nor vex thine ear
With answering wrath more vain than fumes of wine.
I have wronged and yet not wronged thee. Whence or when
Strange whispers rose that turned thy heart from mine
I would not know for shame's sake, Guendolen,
And honour's that I bear thee.

GUENDOLEN.

Didst thou deem

I would outlive with thee the scorn of men,
A slave enthroned beside a traitor? Seem
These eyes and lips and hands of mine a slave's
Uplift for mercy toward thee? Such a dream
Sets realms on fire, and turns their fields to graves.

LOCRINE.

No dream is mine that does thee less than right:
Albeit thy words be wild as warring waves,
I know thee higher of heart than shame could smite
And queenlier than thy queenship.

GUENDOLEN.

Dost the know
What day records to day and night to night -
How he whose wrath was rained as hail or snow
On Troy's adulterous towers, when treacherous flame
Devoured them, and our fathers' roofs lay low,
And all their praise was turned to fire and shame -
All-righteous God, who herds the stars of heaven
As sheep within his sheepfold--God, whose name
Compels the wandering clouds to service, given
As surely as even the sun's is--loves or hates
Treason? He loved our sires: were they forgiven?
Their walls upreared of gods, their sevenfold gates,
Might these keep out his justice? What art thou
To make thy will more strong and sure than fate's?
Thy fate am I, that falls upon thee now.
Wilt thou not slay me yet--and slay thy son?
So shall thy fate change, and unbend the brow
That now looks mortal on thee.

LOCRINE.

What is done
Lies now past help or pleading: nor would I
Plead with thee, knowing that love henceforth is none
Nor trust between us till the day we die.
Yet, if thy name be woman,--if thine heart
Be not burnt up with fire of hell, and lie
Not wounded even to death--albeit we part,
Let there not be between us war, but peace,
Though love may be not.

GUENDOLEN.

Peace? The man thou art
Craves--and shame bids not breath within him cease -
Craves of the woman that thou knowest I am
Peace? Ay, take hands at parting, and release
Each heart, each hand, each other: shall the lamb,
The lamb-like woman, born to cower and bleed,
Withstand his will whose choice may save or damn
Her days and nights, her word and thought and deed -
Take heart to outdare her lord the lion? How
Should this be--if the lion's imperial seed
Life not against his sire as brave a brow
As frowns upon his mother?--Peace be then
Between us: none may stand before thee now:
No son of thine keep faith with Guendolen.

MADAN.

I have held my peace perforce, it seems, too long,
Being slower of speech than sons of meaner men.

But seeing my sire hath done my mother wrong,
My hand is hers to serve against my sire.

GUENDOLEN.

And God shall make thine hand against him strong.

LOCRINE.

Ay: when the hearthstead flames, the roof takes fire.

GUENDOLEN.

Woe worth his hand who set the hearth on flame!

LOCRINE.

Curse not our fathers; though thy fierce desire
Drive thine own son against his father, shame
Should rein thy tongue from speech too shameless.

GUENDOLEN.

Ay!
And thou, my holy-hearted lord,--the same
Whose hand was laid in mine and bound to lie
There fast for ever if faith be found on earth -
If truth be true, and shame not wholly die -
Hast thou not made thy mockery and thy mirth,
Thy laughter and thy scorn, of shame? But we,
Thy wife by wedlock, and thy son by birth,
Who have no part in spirit and soul with thee,
Will bear no part in kingdom nor in life

With one who hath put to shame his child and me.
Thy true-born son, and I that was thy wife,
Will see thee dead or perish. Call thy men
About thee; bid them gird their loins for strife
More dire than theirs who storm the wild wolf's den;
For if thou dare not slay us here today
Thou art dead.

LOCRINE.

Thou knowest I dare not, Guendolen,
Dare what the ravenous beasts whose life is prey
Dream not of doing, though drunk with bloodshed.

GUENDOLEN.

No:
Thou art gentle, and beasts are honest: no such way
Lies open toward thy fearful foot: not so
Shalt thou find surety from these foes of thine.
Woe worth thee therefore! yea, a sevenfold woe
Shall God through us rain down on thee, Locrine.
Hadst thou the heart God hath not given thee--then
Our blood might run before thy feet like wine
And wash thy way toward sin in sight of men
Smooth, soft, and safe. But if thou shed it not -
If Madan live to look on Guendolen
Living--I wot not what shall be--I wot
What shall not--thou shalt have no joy to live
More than have they for whom God's wrath grows hot.

LOCRINE.

God's grace is no such gift as thou canst give,
Queen, or withhold. Farewell.

GUENDOLEN.

I dare not say
Farewell.

LOCRINE.

And why?

GUENDOLEN.

Thou hast not said--Forgive.

LOCRINE.

I say it--I have said. Thou wilt not hear me?

GUENDOLEN.

Nay.
[Exeunt.

ACT V.

SCENE I.--Fields near the Severn.

Enter on one side LOCRINE and his army: on the other side
GUENDOLEN, MADAN, and their army.

LOCRINE.

Stand fast, and sound a parley.

MADAN.

Halt: it seems
They would have rather speech than strokes of us.

LOCRINE.

This light of dawn is like an evil dream's
That comes and goes and is not. Yea, and thus
Our hope on both sides wavering dares allow
No light but fire to bid us die or live.
- Son, and my wife that was, my rebels now,
That here we stand with death to take or give
I call the sun of heaven, God's likeness wrought

On darkness, whence all spirits breathe and shine,
To witness, is no work of will or thought
Conceived or bred in brain or heart of mine.
Ye have levied wars against me, and compelled
My will unwilling and my power withheld
To strike the stroke I would not, when I might.
Will ye not yet take thought, and spare these men
Whom else the blind and burning fire of fight
Must feed upon for pasture? Guendolen,
Had I not left thee queen in Troynovant,
Though wife no more of mine, in all this land
No hand had risen, no eye had glared askant,
Against me: thine is each man's heart and hand
That burns and strikes in all this battle raised
To serve and slake thy vengeance. With my son
I plead not, seeing his praise in arms dispraised
For ever, and his deeds of truth undone
By patricidal treason. But with thee
Peace would I have, if peace again may be
Between us. Blood by wrath unnatural shed
Or spent in civic battle burns the land
Whereon it falls like fire, and brands as red
The conqueror's forehead as the warrior's hand.
I pray thee, spare this people: reign in peace
With separate honours in a several state:
As love that was hath ceased, let hatred cease:
Let not our personal cause be made the fate
That damns to death men innocent, and turns
The joy of life to darkness. Thine alone
Is all this war: to slake the flame that burns
Thus high should crown thee royal, and enthrone
Thy praise in all men's memories. If thou wilt,
Peace let there be: if not, be thine the guilt.

GUENDOLEN.

Mine? Hear it, heaven,--and men, bear witness! Mine
The treachery that hath rent our realm in twain -
Mine, mine the adulterous treason. Not Locrine,
Not he, found loyal to my love in vain,
Hath brought the civic sword and fire of strife
On British fields and homesteads, clothed with joy,
Crowned with content and comfort: I, his wife,
Have brought on Troynovant the fires of Troy.
He lifts his head before the sun of heaven
And swears it--lies, and lives. Is God's bright sword
Broken, wherewith the gates of Troy--the seven
Strong gates that gods who built them held in ward -
Were broken even as wattled reeds with fire?
Son, by what name shall honour call thy sire?

MADAN.

How long shall I and all these mail-clad men
Stand and give ear, or gape and catch at flies,
While ye wage warring words that wound not? When
Have I been found of you so wordy-wise
That thou or he should call to counsel one
So slow of speech and wit as thou and he,
Who know my hand no sluggard, know your son?
Till speech be clothed in iron, bid not me
Speak.

LOCRINE.

Yet he speaks not ill.

GUENDOLEN.

Did I not know
Mine honour perfect as thy shame, Locrine,
Now might I say, and turn to pride my woe,
Mine only were this boy, and none of thine.
But what thou mayest I may not. Where are they
Who ride not with their lord and sire today?
Thy secret Scythian and your changeling child,
Where hide they now their heads that lurk not hidden
There where thy treason deemed them safe, and smiled?
When arms were levied, and thy servants bidden
About thee to withstand the doom of men
Whose loyal angers flamed upon our side
Against thee, from thy smooth-skinned she-wolf's den
Her whelp and she sought covert unespied,
But not from thee far off. Thou hast born them hither
For refuge in this west that stands for thee
Against our cause, whose very name should wither
The hearts of them that hate it. Where is she?
Hath she not heart to keep thy side? or thou,
Dost thou think shame to stand beside her now
And bid her look upon thy son and wife?
Nay, she should ride at thy right hand and laugh
To see so fair a lordly field of strife
Shine for her sake, whose lips thy love bids quaff
For pledge of trustless troth the blood of men.

LOCRINE.

Should I not put her in thine hand to slay?
Hell hath laid hold upon thee, Guendolen,
And turned thine heart to hell-fire. Be thy prey

Thyself, the wolfish huntress: and the blood
Rest on thine head that here shall now be spilt.

GUENDOLEN.

Let it run broader than this water's flood
Swells after storm, it shall not cleanse thy guilt.
Give now the word of charge; and God do right
Between us in the fiery courts of fight.
[Exeunt.

SCENE II.--The banks of the Severn.

Enter ESTRILD and SABRINA.

SABRINA.

When will my father come again?

ESTRILD.

God knows,
Sweet.

SABRINA.

Hast thou seen how wide this water flows -
How smooth it swells and shines from brim to brim,
How fair, how full? Nay, then thine eyes are dim.

Thou dost not weep for fear lest evil men
Or that more evil woman--Guendolen
Didst thou not call her yesternight by name? -
Should put my father's might in arms to shame?
What is she so to levy shameful strife
Against my sire and thee?

ESTRILD.

His wife! his wife!

SABRINA.

Why, that art thou.

ESTRILD

Woe worth me!

SABRINA.

Nay, woe worth
Her wickedness! How may the heavens and earth
Endure her?

ESTRILD.

Heaven is fire, and earth a sword,
Against us.

SABRINA.

May the wife withstand her lord

And war upon him? Nay, no wife is she -
And no true mother thou to mock at me.

ESTRILD.

Yea, no true wife or mother, child, am I.
Yet, child, thou shouldst not say it--and bid me die.

SABRINA.

I bid thee live and laugh at wicked foes
Even as my sire and I do. What! 'God knows,'
Thou sayest, and yet art fearful? Is he not
Righteous, that we should fear to take the lot
Forth of his hand that deals it? And my sire,
Kind as the sun in heaven, and strong as fire,
Hath he not God upon his side and ours,
Even all the gods and stars and all their powers?

ESTRILD.

I know not. Fate at sight of thee should break
His covenant--doom grow gentle for thy sake.

SABRINA.

Wherefore?

ESTRILD.

Because thou knowest not wherefore. Child,
My days were darkened, and the ways were wild
Wherethrough my dark doom led me toward this end,

Ere I beheld thy sire, my lord, my friend,
My king, my stay, my saviour. Let thine hand
Lie still in mine. Thou canst not understand,
Yet would I tell thee somewhat. Ere I knew
If aught of evil or good were false or true,
If aught of life were worth our hope or fear,
There fell on me the fate that sets us here.
For in my father's kingdom oversea -

SABRINA.

Thou wast not born in Britain?

ESTRILD.

Woe is me,
No: happier hap had mine perchance been then.

SABRINA.

And was not I? Are these all stranger men?

ESTRILD.

Ay, wast thou, child--a Briton born: God give
Thy name the grace on British tongues to live!

SABRINA.

Is that so good a gift of God's--to die
And leave a name alive in memory? I
Would rather live this river's life, and be
Held of no less or more account than he.

Lo, how he lives and laughs! and hath no name,
Thou sayest--or one forgotten even of fame
That lives on poor men's lips and falters down
To nothing. But thy father? and his crown?
Did he less hate the coil of it than mine,
Or love thee less--nay, then he were not thine -
Than he, my sire, loves me?

ESTRILD.

And wilt thou hear
All? Child, my child, love born of love, more dear
Than very love was ever! Hearken then.
This plague, this fire, that hunts us--Guendolen -
Was wedded to thy sire ere I and he
Cast ever eyes on either. Woe is me!
Thou canst not dream, sweet, what my soul would say
And not affright thee.

SABRINA.

Thou affright me? Nay,
Mock not. This evil woman--when he knew
Thee, this my sweet good mother, wise and true -
He cast from him and hated.

ESTRILD.

Yea--and now
For that shall haply he and I and thou
Die.

SABRINA.

What is death? I never saw his face
That I should fear it.

ESTRILD.

Whether grief or grace
Or curse or blessing breathe from it, and give
Aught worse or better than the life we live,
I know no more than thou knowest; perchance,
Less. When we sleep, they say, or fall in trance,
We die awhile. Well spake thine innocent breath -
I THINK THERE IS NO DEATH BUT FEAR OF DEATH.

SABRINA.

Did I say this? but that was long ago -
Months. Now I know not--yet I think I know -
Whether I fear or fear not it. Hard by
Men fight even now--they strike and kill and die
Red-handed; nay, we hear the roar and see
The lightning of the battle: can it be
That what no soul of all these brave men fears
Should sound so fearful save in foolish ears?
But all this while I know not where it lay,
Thy father's kingdom.

ESTRILD.

Far from here away
It lies beyond the wide waste water's bound
That clasps with bitter waves this sweet land round.

Thou hast seen the great sea never, nor canst dream
How fairer far than earth's most lordly stream
It rolls its royal waters here and there,
Most glorious born of all things anywhere,
Most fateful and most godlike; fit to make
Men love life better for the sweet sight's sake
And less fear death if death for them should be
Shrined in the sacred splendours of the sea
As God in heaven s mid mystery. Night and day
Forth of my tower-girt homestead would I stray
To gaze thereon as thou upon the bright
Soft river whence thy soul took less delight
Than mine of the outer sea, albeit I know
How great thy joy was of it. Now--for so
The high gods willed it should be--once at morn
Strange men there landing bore me thence forlorn
Across the wan wild waters in their bark,
I wist not where, through change of light and dark,
Till their fierce lord, the son of spoil and strife,
Made me by forceful marriage-rites his wife.
Then sailed they toward the white and flower-sweet strand
Whose free folk follow on thy father's hand,
And warred against him, slaying his brother: and he
Hurled all their force back hurtling toward the sea,
And slew my lord their king; but me he gave
Grace, and received not as a wandering slave,
But one whom seeing he loved for pity: why
Should else a sad strange woman such as I
Find in his fair sight favour? and for me
He built the bower wherein I bare him thee,
And whence but now he hath brought us westward, here
To abide the extreme of utmost hope or fear.
And come what end may ever, death or life,

I live or die, if truth be truth, his wife;
And none but I and thou, though day wax dim,
Though night grow strong, hath any part in him.

SABRINA.

What should we fear, then? whence might any
Fall on us?

ESTRILD.

Ah! Ah me! God answers here.

Enter LOCRINE, wounded.

LOCRINE.

Praised be the gods who have brought me safe--to die
Beside thee. Nay, but kneel not--rise, and fly
Ere death take hold on thee too. Bid the child
Kiss me. The ways all round are wide and wild -
Ye may win safe away. They deemed me dead -
My last friends left--who saw me fallen, and fled
No shame is theirs--they fought to the end. But ye,
Fly: not your love can keep my life in me -
Not even the sight and sense of you so near.

SABRINA.

How can we fly, father?

ESTRILD.

She would not fear -
Thy very child is she--no heart less high
Than thine sustains her--and we will not fly.

LOCRINE.

So shall their work be perfect. Yea, I know
Our fate is fallen upon us, and its woe.
Yet have we lacked not gladness--and this end
Is not so hard. We have had sweet life to friend,
And find not death our enemy. All men born
Die, and but few find evening one with morn
As I do, seeing the sun of all my life
Lighten my death in sight of child and wife.
I would not live again to lose that kiss,
And die some death not half so sweet as this.
[Dies.

ESTRILD.

Thou thought'st to cleave in twain my life and
To cast my hand away in death, Locrine?
See now if death have drawn thee far from me!
[Stabs herself.

SABRINA.

Thou diest, and hast not slain me, mother?

ESTRILD.

Thee?
Forgive me, child! and so may they forgive.
[Dies.

SABRINA.

O mother, canst thou die and bid me live?

Enter GUENDOLEN, MADAN, and Soldiers.

GUENDOLEN.

Dead? Ah! my traitor with his harlot fled
Hellward?

MADAN.

Their child is left thee.

GUENDOLEN.

She! not dead?

SABRINA.

Thou hast slain my mother and sire--thou hast slain thy lord -
Strike now, and slay me.

GUENDOLEN.

Smite her with thy sword.

MADAN.

I know not if I dare. I dare not.

GUENDOLEN.

Shame
Consume thee!--Thou--what call they, girl, thy name?
Daughter of Estrild,--daughter of Locrine, -
Daughter of death and darkness!

SABRINA.

Yet not thine.
Darkness and death are come on us, and thou,
Whose servants are they: heaven behind thee now
Stands, and withholds the thunder: yet on me
He gives thee not, who helps and comforts thee,
Power for one hour of darkness. Ere thine hand
Can put forth power to slay me where I stand
Safe shall I sleep as these that here lie slain.

GUENDOLEN.

She dares not--though the heart in her be fain,
The flesh draws back for fear. She dares not.

SABRINA.

See!
I change no more of warring words with thee
O father, O my mother, here am I:
They hurt me not who can but bid me die.

[She leaps into the river.

GUENDOLEN.

Save her! God pardon me!

MADAN.

The water whirls
Down out of sight her tender face, and hurls
Her soft light limbs to deathward. God forgive -
Thee, sayest thou, mother? Wouldst thou bid her live?

GUENDOLEN.

What have we done?

MADAN.

The work we came to do.
That God, thou said'st, should stand for judge of you
Whose judgment smote with mortal fire and sword
Troy, for such cause as bade thee slay thy lord.
Now, as between his fathers and their foes
The lord of gods dealt judgment, winged with woes
And girt about with ruin, hath he sent
On these destruction.

GUENDOLEN.

Yea.

MADAN.

Art thou content?

GUENDOLEN.

The gods are wise who lead us--now to smite,
And now to spare: we dwell but in their sigh
And work but what their will is. What hath been
Is past. But these, that once were king and queen,
The sun, that feeds on death, shall not consume
Naked. Not I would sunder tomb from tomb
Of these twain foes of mine, in death made one -
I, that when darkness hides me from the sun
Shall sleep alone, with none to rest by me.
But thou--this one time more I look on thee -
Fair face, brave hand, weak heart that wast not mine -
Sleep sound--and God be good to thee, Locrine.
I was not. She was fair as heaven in spring
Whom thou didst love indeed. Sleep, queen and king,
Forgiven; and if--God knows--being dead, ye live,
And keep remembrance yet of me--forgive.

[Exeunt.

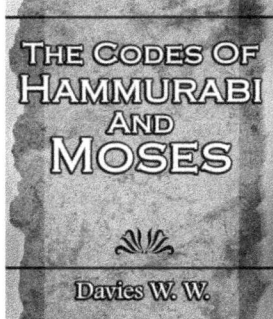

The Codes Of Hammurabi And Moses
W. W. Davies

QTY

The discovery of the Hammurabi Code is one of the greatest achievements of archaeology, and is of paramount interest, not only to the student of the Bible, but also to all those interested in ancient history...

Religion   **ISBN:** *1-59462-338-4*   **Pages:132**
MSRP $12.95

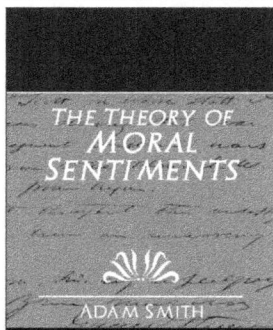

The Theory of Moral Sentiments
Adam Smith

QTY

This work from 1749. contains original theories of conscience amd moral judgment and it is the foundation for systemof morals.

Philosophy **ISBN:** *1-59462-777-0*   **Pages:536**
MSRP $19.95

Jessica's First Prayer
Hesba Stretton

QTY

In a screened and secluded corner of one of the many railway-bridges which span the streets of London there could be seen a few years ago, from five o'clock every morning until half past eight, a tidily set-out coffee-stall, consisting of a trestle and board, upon which stood two large tin cans, with a small fire of charcoal burning under each so as to keep the coffee boiling during the early hours of the morning when the work-people were thronging into the city on their way to their daily toil...

Pages:84

Childrens **ISBN:** *1-59462-373-2*   **MSRP $9.95**

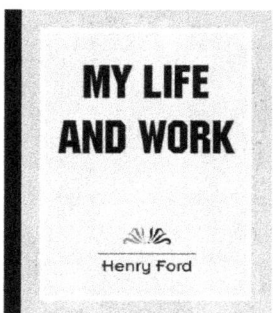

My Life and Work
Henry Ford

QTY

Henry Ford revolutionized the world with his implementation of mass production for the Model T automobile. Gain valuable business insight into his life and work with his own auto-biography... "We have only started on our development of our country we have not as yet, with all our talk of wonderful progress, done more than scratch the surface. The progress has been wonderful enough but..."

Pages:300

Biographies/   **ISBN:** *1-59462-198-5*   **MSRP $21.95**

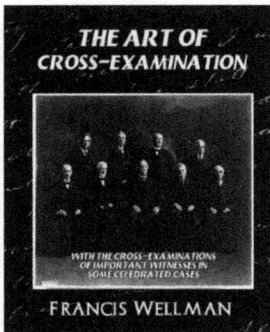

The Art of Cross-Examination
Francis Wellman

QTY

I presume it is the experience of every author, after his first book is published upon an important subject, to be almost overwhelmed with a wealth of ideas and illustrations which could readily have been included in his book, and which to his own mind, at least, seem to make a second edition inevitable. Such certainly was the case with me; and when the first edition had reached its sixth impression in five months, I rejoiced to learn that it seemed to my publishers that the book had met with a sufficiently favorable reception to justify a second and considerably enlarged edition. ..

Reference   **ISBN: *1-59462-647-2***   **Pages:412**

MSRP $19.95

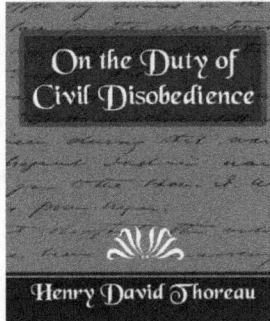

On the Duty of Civil Disobedience
Henry David Thoreau

QTY

Thoreau wrote his famous essay, On the Duty of Civil Disobedience, as a protest against an unjust but popular war and the immoral but popular institution of slave-owning. He did more than write—he declined to pay his taxes, and was hauled off to gaol in consequence. Who can say how much this refusal of his hastened the end of the war and of slavery ?

Law   **ISBN: *1-59462-747-9***   **Pages:48**

MSRP $7.45

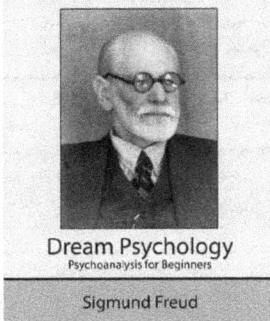

Dream Psychology Psychoanalysis for Beginners
Sigmund Freud

QTY

Sigmund Freud, born Sigismund Schlomo Freud (May 6, 1856 - September 23, 1939), was a Jewish-Austrian neurologist and psychiatrist who co-founded the psychoanalytic school of psychology. Freud is best known for his theories of the unconscious mind, especially involving the mechanism of repression; his redefinition of sexual desire as mobile and directed towards a wide variety of objects; and his therapeutic techniques, especially his understanding of transference in the therapeutic relationship and the presumed value of dreams as sources of insight into unconscious desires.

Psychology   **ISBN: *1-59462-905-6***   **Pages:196**

MSRP $15.45

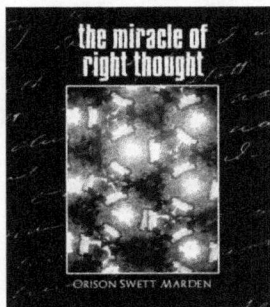

The Miracle of Right Thought
Orison Swett Marden

QTY

Believe with all of your heart that you will do what you were made to do. When the mind has once formed the habit of holding cheerful, happy, prosperous pictures, it will not be easy to form the opposite habit. It does not matter how improbable or how far away this realization may see, or how dark the prospects may be, if we visualize them as best we can, as vividly as possible, hold tenaciously to them and vigorously struggle to attain them, they will gradually become actualized, realized in the life. But a desire, a longing without endeavor, a yearning abandoned or held indifferently will vanish without realization.

Self Help   **ISBN: *1-59462-644-8***   **Pages:360**

MSRP $25.45

QTY

The Rosicrucian Cosmo-Conception Mystic Christianity *by Max Heindel*   ISBN: *1-59462-188-8*   **$38.95**
The Rosicrucian Cosmo-conception is not dogmatic, neither does it appeal to any other authority than the reason of the student. It is: not controversial, but is: sent forth in the, hope that it may help to clear...   New Age/Religion Pages 646

Abandonment To Divine Providence *by Jean-Pierre de Caussade*   ISBN: *1-59462-228-0*   **$25.95**
"The Rev. Jean Pierre de Caussade was one of the most remarkable spiritual writers of the Society of Jesus in France in the 18th Century. His death took place at Toulouse in 1751. His works have gone through many editions and have been republished...   Inspirational/Religion Pages 400

Mental Chemistry *by Charles Haanel*   ISBN: *1-59462-192-6*   **$23.95**
Mental Chemistry allows the change of material conditions by combining and appropriately utilizing the power of the mind. Much like applied chemistry creates something new and unique out of careful combinations of chemicals the mastery of mental chemistry...   New Age Pages 354

The Letters of Robert Browning and Elizabeth Barret Barrett 1845-1846 vol II   ISBN: *1-59462-193-4*   **$35.95**
by Robert Browning and Elizabeth Barrett   Biographies Pages 596

Gleanings In Genesis (volume I) *by Arthur W. Pink*   ISBN: *1-59462-130-6*   **$27.45**
Appropriately has Genesis been termed "the seed plot of the Bible" for in it we have, in germ form, almost all of the great doctrines which are afterwards fully developed in the books of Scripture which follow...   Religion/Inspirational Pages 420

The Master Key *by L. W. de Laurence*   ISBN: *1-59462-001-6*   **$30.95**
In no branch of human knowledge has there been a more lively increase of the spirit of research during the past few years than in the study of Psychology, Concentration and Mental Discipline. The requests for authentic lessons in Thought Control, Mental Discipline and...   New Age/Business Pages 422

The Lesser Key Of Solomon Goetia *by L. W. de Laurence*   ISBN: *1-59462-092-X*   **$9.95**
This translation of the first book of the "Lernegton" which is now for the first time made accessible to students of Talismanic Magic was done, after careful collation and edition, from numerous Ancient Manuscripts in Hebrew, Latin, and French...   New Age/Occult Pages 92

Rubaiyat Of Omar Khayyam *by Edward Fitzgerald*   ISBN:*1-59462-332-5*   **$13.95**
Edward Fitzgerald, whom the world has already learned, in spite of his own efforts to remain within the shadow of anonymity, to look upon as one of the rarest poets of the century, was born at Bredfield, in Suffolk, on the 31st of March, 1809. He was the third son of John Purcell...   Music Pages 172

Ancient Law *by Henry Maine*   ISBN: *1-59462-128-4*   **$29.95**
The chief object of the following pages is to indicate some of the earliest ideas of mankind, as they are reflected in Ancient Law, and to point out the relation of those ideas to modern thought.   Religion/History Pages 452

Far-Away Stories *by William J. Locke*   ISBN: *1-59462-129-2*   **$19.45**
"Good wine needs no bush, but a collection of mixed vintages does. And this book is just such a collection. Some of the stories I do not want to remain buried for ever in the museum files of dead magazine-numbers an author's not unpardonable vanity..."   Fiction Pages 272

Life of David Crockett *by David Crockett*   ISBN: *1-59462-250-7*   **$27.45**
"Colonel David Crockett was one of the most remarkable men of the times in which he lived. Born in humble life, but gifted with a strong will, an indomitable courage, and unremitting perseverance...   Biographies/New Age Pages 424

Lip-Reading *by Edward Nitchie*   ISBN: *1-59462-206-X*   **$25.95**
Edward B. Nitchie, founder of the New York School for the Hard of Hearing, now the Nitchie School of Lip-Reading, Inc, wrote "LIP-READING Principles and Practice". The development and perfecting of this meritorious work on lip-reading was an undertaking...   How-to Pages 400

A Handbook of Suggestive Therapeutics, Applied Hypnotism, Psychic Science   ISBN: *1-59462-214-0*   **$24.95**
by Henry Munro   Health/New Age/Health/Self-help Pages 376

A Doll's House: and Two Other Plays *by Henrik Ibsen*   ISBN: *1-59462-112-8*   **$19.95**
Henrik Ibsen created this classic when in revolutionary 1848 Rome. Introducing some striking concepts in playwriting for the realist genre, this play has been studied the world over.   Fiction/Classics/Plays 308

The Light of Asia *by sir Edwin Arnold*   ISBN: *1-59462-204-3*   **$13.95**
In this poetic masterpiece, Edwin Arnold describes the life and teachings of Buddha. The man who was to become known as Buddha to the world was born as Prince Gautama of India but he rejected the worldly riches and abandoned the reigns of power when...   Religion/History/Biographies Pages 170

The Complete Works of Guy de Maupassant *by Guy de Maupassant*   ISBN: *1-59462-157-8*   **$16.95**
"For days and days, nights and nights, I had dreamed of that first kiss which was to consecrate our engagement, and I knew not on what spot I should put my lips..."   Fiction/Classics Pages 240

The Art of Cross-Examination *by Francis L. Wellman*   ISBN: *1-59462-309-0*   **$26.95**
Written by a renowned trial lawyer, Wellman imparts his experience and uses case studies to explain how to use psychology to extract desired information through questioning.   How-to/Science/Reference Pages 408

Answered or Unanswered? *by Louisa Vaughan*   ISBN: *1-59462-248-5*   **$10.95**
Miracles of Faith in China   Religion Pages 112

The Edinburgh Lectures on Mental Science (1909) *by Thomas*   ISBN: *1-59462-008-3*   **$11.95**
This book contains the substance of a course of lectures recently given by the writer in the Queen Street Hall, Edinburgh. Its purpose is to indicate the Natural Principles governing the relation between Mental Action and Material Conditions...   New Age/Psychology Pages 148

Ayesha *by H. Rider Haggard*   ISBN: *1-59462-301-5*   **$24.95**
Verily and indeed it is the unexpected that happens! Probably if there was one person upon the earth from whom the Editor of this, and of a certain previous history, did not expect to hear again...   Classics Pages 380

Ayala's Angel *by Anthony Trollope*   ISBN: *1-59462-352-X*   **$29.95**
The two girls were both pretty, but Lucy who was twenty-one who supposed to be simple and comparatively unattractive, whereas Ayala was credited, as her Bombwhat romantic name might show, with poetic charm and a taste for romance. Ayala when her father died was nineteen...   Fiction Pages 484

The American Commonwealth *by James Bryce*   ISBN: *1-59462-286-8*   **$34.45**
An interpretation of American democratic political theory. It examines political mechanics and society from the perspective of Scotsman James Bryce   Politics Pages 572

Stories of the Pilgrims *by Margaret P. Pumphrey*   ISBN: *1-59462-116-0*   **$17.95**
This book explores pilgrims religious oppression in England as well as their escape to Holland and eventual crossing to America on the Mayflower, and their early days in New England...   History Pages 268

www.bookjungle.com *email: sales@bookjungle.com fax: 630-214-0564 mail: Book Jungle PO Box 2226 Champaign, IL 61825*

QTY

The Fasting Cure *by Sinclair Upton*　　　　　　　　　ISBN: *1-59462-222-1*　**$13.95**
In the Cosmopolitan Magazine for May, 1910, and in the Contemporary Review (London) for April, 1910, I published an article dealing with my experiences in fasting. I have written a great many magazine articles, but never one which attracted so much attention... New Age/Self Help/Health Pages 164

Hebrew Astrology *by Sepharial*　　　　　　　　　　ISBN: *1-59462-308-2*　**$13.45**
In these days of advanced thinking it is a matter of common observation that we have left many of the old landmarks behind and that we are now pressing forward to greater heights and to a wider horizon than that which represented the mind-content of our progenitors... Astrology Pages 144

Thought Vibration or The Law of Attraction in the Thought World　　ISBN: *1-59462-127-6*　**$12.95**

by William Walker Atkinson　　　　　　　　　　　　　　　*Psychology/Religion Pages 144*

Optimism *by Helen Keller*　　　　　　　　　　　ISBN: *1-59462-108-X*　**$15.95**
Helen Keller was blind, deaf, and mute since 19 months old, yet famously learned how to overcome these handicaps, communicate with the world, and spread her lectures promoting optimism. An inspiring read for everyone... Biographies/Inspirational Pages 84

Sara Crewe *by Frances Burnett*　　　　　　　　　ISBN: *1-59462-360-0*　**$9.45**
In the first place, Miss Minchin lived in London. Her home was a large, dull, tall one, in a large, dull square, where all the houses were alike, and all the sparrows were alike, and where all the door-knockers made the same heavy sound... Childrens/Classic Pages 88

The Autobiography of Benjamin Franklin *by Benjamin Franklin*　　ISBN: *1-59462-135-7*　**$24.95**
The Autobiography of Benjamin Franklin has probably been more extensively read than any other American historical work, and no other book of its kind has had such ups and downs of fortune. Franklin lived for many years in England, where he was agent... Biographies/History Pages 332

Name	
Email	
Telephone	
Address	
City, State ZIP	

☐ **Credit Card**　　　　　☐ **Check / Money Order**

Credit Card Number	
Expiration Date	
Signature	

Please Mail to:　Book Jungle
PO Box 2226
Champaign, IL 61825
or Fax to:　　　630-214-0564

ORDERING INFORMATION

web*: www.bookjungle.com*
email*: sales@bookjungle.com*
fax*: 630-214-0564*
mail*: Book Jungle PO Box 2226 Champaign, IL 61825*
or PayPal *to sales@bookjungle.com*

Please contact us for bulk discounts

DIRECT-ORDER TERMS

**20% Discount if You Order
Two or More Books**
Free Domestic Shipping!
Accepted: Master Card, Visa,
Discover, American Express

www.ingramcontent.com/pod-product-compliance
Lightning Source LLC
Chambersburg PA
CBHW081231090426
42738CB00016B/3258